THE BOOK OF OLD SHIPS

FROM EGYPTIAN GALLEYS TO CLIPPER SHIPS

HENRY B. CULVER

ILLUSTRATED BY
GORDON GRANT

DOVER PUBLICATIONS, INC.
NEW YORK

To THOSE unknown craftsmen and mariners upon whose skill and seamanship is founded the progress of ship-building through the ages; to the memory of the known illustrious designers, master shipwrights and artists of a later day, Pett, Shish, Puget; to the projectors and builders of the frigates, packets and clippers of our own era, Humphrey, Griffith, and MacKay, and to all lovers of ships, be they mariners or landlubbers, this book is humbly and affectionately dedicated.

Published in Canada by General Publishing Company, Ltd., 30 Lesmill Road, Don Mills, Toronto, Ontario.

This Dover edition, first published in 1992, is an unabridged, slightly corrected republication of the Flotilla Edition (750 numbered copies) of the work originally published by Doubleday, Page and Company, Garden City, New York in 1924 under the title, *The Book of Old Ships: And Something of Their Evolution and Romance/Wherein will be found* drawings *and* descriptions *of many varieties of* vessels, *both long and round, showing their development from most remote times; the* portraiture of their progress, *their garnishment, etc., etc., etc./Together with* DIVERS DISSERTATIONS *upon the* Origins of Shipping; *also an* APPENDIX *wherein will be discovered to the* inquisitive *much information appertaining to the* ANCIENT USES *and* customs of the sea *and* mariners/*Illustrated with a variety of original designs of shipping compiled from authentic sources.* The illustration on page vi originally appeared in color. Some of the material in this edition has been moved from the original locations.

DOVER *Pictorial Archive* SERIES

Manufactured in the United States of America
Dover Publications, Inc., 31 East 2nd Street, Mineola, N.Y. 11501

Library of Congress Cataloging in Publication Data

Culver, Henry B. (Henry Brundage), b. 1869.
[Book of old ships and something of their evolution and romance]
The book of old ships : from Egyptian galleys to clipper ships / Henry B. Culver ; illustrated by Gordon Grant.
        p.   cm. — (Dover pictorial archive series)
Originally published: The book of old ships and something of their evolution and romance. Garden City, N.Y. : Doubleday, Page, 1924.
Includes bibliographical references.
ISBN 0-486-27332-6 (pbk.)
1. Shipbuilding—History.   I. Grant, Gordon, 1875–1962.   II. Title.   III. Series.
VM15.C9   1992
387.2'1—dc20   92-21987
                                                                                   CIP

CONTENTS

PART I

LONG SHIPS

PART II

ROUND SHIPS

CONTENTS

CONTENTS

APPENDIX

. . . . "Whom once men tended like a queen . . . Let be . . .
She is one with all things that have been—"

PREFACE

NAVIGATION by man of the waterways of the earth is believably co-eval with his earliest activities. The scientists tell us that his life was then nomadic. In the course of his migrations in search of food or more congenial conditions of climate, he would of necessity have met with bodies of water too deep or too wide to be crossed by fording or swimming. In fishing and in hunting, too, he would employ the most primitive form of aquatic conveyance—a floating log. As the next step he would naturally join several logs together by means of wythes or creeping plants, thus enabling him to float dry shod. The difference between this, the simplest form of marine construction, the raft, and the greatest ocean leviathan of to-day is one of degree only.

Supported by his log or seated upon his raft, the next question was one of propulsion; a paddle of a flattened piece of wood was, after hand and foot, the obvious answer. Soon the problem demanded the invention of a means of directing the unwieldy craft; a similar paddle used as a rudder was the solution. Immediately the presence of a further factor, the effect of the wind upon the floating mass, became evident. Paddling with a favouring breeze was manifestly easier than with none or against a contrary one. Perhaps, originally a bough extending up into the air from the log,

or the increased velocity of his raft when an erect position
thereon offered a greater resistance to the wind, served to
call attention to the aid offered by such an obstruction. To
the simple but reasoning mind of the man-animal, such
assistance could not be disregarded upon the next voyage.
Ultimately, from the skin of some wild beast, man devised
his first harness for the wind, a sail.

Ages before the existence of any pictorial or written evidence which has survived to our day man had devised and
developed to a high degree of perfection a fabricated boat
propelled by both oars and sail. The process, a slow one,
was one of evolution, a theory as firmly established and as applicable to the creatures of the brain of man as man's brain
itself. One of the first marine inventions, the paddle, ex-
hausted the possibilities of that object in certain respects.
Witness its survival in practically primordial form until to-
day as the implement best adapted to secure the most satisfactory results in the propulsion of primitive narrow water
craft. Of these the canoe typifies the almost universal persistence of a boat fashioned from a hollowed-out log sharp-
ened at both ends.

But the paddle was susceptible of further development
under other conditions, namely, where the width of the craft
provided the means of employing the principle of the lever;
hence the oar with its oarlock or thole-pin acting as fulcrum.
And this device by the alteration of the position of the fulcrum and of the point of application of the power possessed
in the form of the paddle wheel and screw propeller, still
further opportunities for improvement. Instances of the

evolution of various parts of the ship might be multiplied indefinitely.   But this work is not intended to be either an historical or a scientific treatise in the strict acceptance of these terms.   It will be scientific in the sense that it will seek for its foundation ascertainable facts, and historic in that it will endeavour to expose the development of certain types of sailing craft from the time of their earliest appearance in pictorial and written annals to the point of attainment of their most significant form.   How far that will be in point of time depends both on the type and on the persistence of some of their most characteristic features.

Nor can it hope to tell in full the story of ancient shipping—the monumental extent of such an undertaking surpassed the untiring research of that profound student of marine archæology, August Jal, and in fact surpassed the measure of his life.   Such a work still remains to be written and will require the combined efforts of a group of collaborators working for many years.   Nor is it to be historical as recording, to any extent, events or acts occurring to the men who trod the decks of the vessels herein to be portrayed.   But there are events and acts intimately connected with ships themselves, events and acts which, had it not been for the ships, would never have come to pass.   These deeds are those which add to the romance of the ship, which fire the imagination and quicken the pulses.

There are many landsmen who love ships with a strange devotion, a devotion not peculiar to men who go down to the sea in ships, an admiration not depending either on the construction of hull, the form of rigging and sails, or on the brains and brawn of those who direct the vessels' paths across the great deep. Their love is founded upon something more intangible and wonderful. It is to be found in that subtle awakening of mental processes, that consciousness of self-appreciation arising from the realization that the object of their affection and interest, the ship, combines all the elements of æsthetic fundamentals; that it is in fact inherently a work of art, replete with line, colour, form, atmosphere. And for the perfect setting of this work of art, intensifying its beauty and romance, is the ever-present, ever-changing mystery of the sea.

It has been thought best not to try to include in the body of the work reproductions of pictorial data and written descriptions upon which several of the types of vessels hereinafter depicted have been based. In the case of all types of vessels of which no reasonably accurate representation is known to exist, each illustration is an attempt to give as rational a depiction of such a vessel as it would appear to us to-day as is possible from the sources of information at hand. In other words, these old ships are presented through the eyes of a 20th Century illustrator in the form modern research gives them, rejecting the trammels of early convention and the naïveté of the ancient contemporary artist.

The text in nearly every instance has been designed as nearly as possible to serve as a commentary upon the illustrations, and to give the reader some idea of the approximate dates when such vessels appeared, flourished, became obsolete, or disappeared. In many instances it has been possible to give some information as to the derivations of the names of the several types of vessels. If the text writer has at times departed from this fixed formula and permitted himself to indulge in some (perhaps) justifiable rhapsodizing, it must be claimed in extenuation that both he and the artist are riding their favourite hobby and that even sea horses are at times liable to become skittish.

The appendix contains some matters which could not be conveniently included in the body of text. Their close association, nevertheless, seemed to render it advisable not to omit them from a work of which their romantic and artistic qualities admittedly make them a part. It was quite impossible without unduly enlarging the scope of the work to include many engaging and desirable lines of discussion.

The notes (necessary evils) have also been relegated to a limbo as far removed from the text as possible, where they may suffer in darkness their penalty unless translated thence by the intercession of some compassionate redeemer.

The author is indebted to several gentlemen whose names have been frequently used in this work: To Mr. R. C. Anderson, Mr. R. Morton Nance, and Mr. G. C. E. Crone, whose contributions to the *Mariner's Mirror*, and personal assistance on points of doubt, have been of the utmost value; thanks are also due to Messrs. L. G. Carr-Laughton, H. S. Vaughan, H. H. Brindley, Commander C. N. Robinson, E. Keble Chatterton, Dr. Jules Sottas, and several others from whose writings quotations have been made and much valuable information obtained.

"An' I don't care if it's North or South,
   The Trades or the China Sea,
Shortened down or everything set —
   Close-hauled or running free —
You paint me a ship as is *like* a ship . . .
   An' *that'll* do for me."

— C. Fox Smith

INTRODUCTION

THE vessels of former times may be roughly classed in two main groups: long ships and round ships. The former, as their name implies, were all those whose length bore a larger proportion to their width than did the round ships. The long ships were usually equipped with both oars and sails, but some types, like the dromon of the early centuries of the Christian era, is said to have been propelled by oars alone. Likewise, the round ship, while depending principally upon sails for motive power, was often equipped with oars as an auxiliary means of propulsion when the wind failed or was unfavourable. Necessarily these two classes intermingled, some examples partaking somewhat of the characteristics of both, so that it is sometimes difficult to differentiate between the two.

The term "nef" was applied quite generally to nearly all vessels, although it is probable that when we find the word used in mediæval times it referred to the larger types of sailing craft. Carrack was a term usually applied to a large vessel. All early nautical terminology is much confused, as one may readily observe by consulting the more ancient writers on marine subjects. Words employed at one period in describing certain types of vessel were applied to quite dissimilar vessels at other times, and the same looseness of terminology obtained in the use of similar or identical terms in different localities in describing quite dissimilar types of craft. The word "galley" may be safely adopted to describe that form of long ship chiefly depending upon oars but equipped with sail as an auxiliary means of propulsion. This type is however frequently alluded to as a "ship," a term in its technical sense restricted to-day to designate a vessel having three or more masts, upon all of which square sails are carried.

Many other names were used to designate vessels of the galley type, such as the words "serpent" and "dragon" in northern Europe, while in the enclosed seas of the south in early times, bireme, trireme, etc., were the names applied to the larger vessels of this class. Examples could be multiplied.

Too much caution cannot be observed in placing dependence upon either the ancient marine pictures or the early writings on naval subjects. Few of either the artists or writers of those days were seamen or even reasonably well versed in marine matters. Besides being ignorant, the ancient writer was always prone to exaggerate. As for the artists, one is inclined to think that, according to their lights, most of them drew approximately what they actually saw, as they saw it, for it may be safely asserted that the minds of the men of antiquity and of the Renaissance period did not react to the stimuli of impressions and sensations received from the objective world exactly as our minds react to them to-day. Many of their representations of round ships may seem to us bizarre. There is, nevertheless, a substantial agreement in most of their depictions of these vessels. The marked differentiation of that class from the galley, when both these classes appear in the same ancient picture, leads to the inevitable conclusion that the old-time draughtsmen could not have seen correctly as to the galley and misrepresented the form of the round ship. Because the galleys as there shown agree in form to the galleys of a much later date, and we know that in this class of vessel there was little change during many centuries.

It is unfortunate that on an important occasion naval archæologists of two Romance countries should have committed an unfortunate mistake. And this in the face of indisputable evidence as to the facts.

The result has been that in the supposed replica sent to the Chicago World's Fair of 1892, in both modern pictorial representations and in recently built models, the *Santa Maria*, the principal "nef" or "nao" of Columbus, has been presented as a perfectly good late 16th Century ship. A further reference to this subject will be found in the body of the work.

One of the corollaries which might be drawn from the efforts of these gentlemen would be that there was no advance or evolution in the form of the round ship between the days of Columbus and those of Drake; which is absurd.

The law of evolution developed at an early date the long ship to a high degree of perfection and in almost unaltered form it persisted for many centuries. The development of the round ship was much slower, but in its later stages infinitely greater and higher than was possible in the galley.

INTRODUCTION

Under the impetus of the Renaissance after the long lethargy of the Dark Ages, naval architecture, beginning in the 16th Century, advanced practically abreast the other sciences. And the end is not yet.

PART I
LONG SHIPS

THE BOOK OF OLD SHIPS

GALLEYS

THE galley was one of the earliest types of vessel. Its existence antedates all historical records. Oars were its principal dependence for motive power, and sail was originally employed only with a favouring breeze. Its form was primarily long and narrow as best suited for propulsion by rowers. Its simplicity of form has been one of its chief reasons of permanency.

Jal, whose name will be often used and from whose writings liberal quotations will be made in this work, in his "Glossaire Nautique" devotes several pages to the presumptive derivation of the word "galley"—*gallée,* in the old French, modern French *galère;* and after dismissing several sources as ridiculous, gives as the most satisfactory origin, the Greek word γαλέια, meaning a rowing vessel.

As distinguished from the ancient round ship whose proportions were about two and one half to three times as long as it was wide, the proportion of the length of the galley to its breadth or beam was as five, six, seven, eight, or even as nine is to one.

As oars gradually displaced paddles and the size of rowing vessels increased, it became necessary to extend the fulcrum so as to facilitate the employment of longer oars. For this purpose an outboard platform or gallery called "apostis" was constructed along the side of the vessel. It provided also a greater space for free circulation along the longitudinal axis of the craft inboard from the oarsmen, as well as for the more convenient and useful disposition of the rowing benches.

This arrangement was chiefly employed in the galleys of the southern European countries. The gallery or apostis seems not to have been adopted generally in northern ships. The loose-footed square sail, extended upon the single yard of early times, was later replaced by one or two lateen sails and it is in this form that we trace the galley to the date of its practical disappearance from Mediterranean waters in the late 18th Century, although a few specimens seem to have survived until as late as 1805. The speed of the galley when rowed and the fact that it could manoeuvre in a calm made it the chief instrument of naval warfare from the most remote past until a considerable time after the use of gunpowder by the Western World. The early galleys of the Mediterranean countries, armed with their deadly metal or metal-sheathed beaks, and propelled by scores of oars in the hands of highly trained and well-disciplined rowers, sought to gain their first advantage by ramming their adversaries. The shock of the impact was terrific and often must have been almost as disastrous to the attacker as to the attacked. When this coup failed, boarding was resorted to. Extending from the vessel's side the apostis offered a more easy access to the attacking forces. The ancient Roman galleys had wooden drawbridges raised vertically upon the sides so arranged that they could be dropped upon the deck of an enemy. Spikes extending from the under side, striking with the full force of the weight of the falling structure, effectively grappled or fastened together the two contending vessels and provided the means of engagement in a body-to-body combat. Military tops, after the yards had been lowered (for these vessels almost always furled sail before engaging), gave a position from which darts, stones, and flaming liquids could be projected down the enemy's decks. The carnage in these ancient sea fights was frightful.

Much nonsense has been written concerning the supposed arrangements of the oars in the larger ancient galleys. And it is one of the curious commentaries upon either the accuracy of the descriptive powers of the ancient writers or upon the apparent lack of understanding of their subsequent translators and would-be elucidators, that the question has never been satisfactorily settled.

Many ingenious theories have been advanced, some ludicrously impossible from purely physical standpoints.

It is not the intention to discuss here any of these attempted explanations or to comment upon the etymological and grammatical discussions upon which most of them are based, but it may be safely stated that not more than two rows of oars could be successfully superposed vertically on separate decks. Recent opinion is that the trireme, the war vessel most employed in early times by the Mediterranean nations, and the most highly developed, was operated by oars extending from the vessel's side in groups or sets of three, emerging from practically the same oar port or opening and operated against three separate thole pins, or through openings separated by not more than a foot in the horizontal plane, each successively higher by a few inches. Such an arrangement applied to a bireme may be seen in the pediment of that masterpiece of classic sculpture known as the Winged Victory of Samothrace. In said pediment, two depressions each about eight inches long by three inches high show where the oar blades were intended to be thrust through the openings in the overhang of the apostis. This plan might have been developed to the limit of its physical possibilities. The theory is plausible and offers an explanation to many supposed and actual difficulties, besides being easily reconciled, it is claimed, with many of the more baffling points in the texts of the ancient writers. Be this as it may, the form of galley which we know from reliable pictorial descriptions and from actual examples, the galley of almost our own day, had only one row of oars all in the same place.

But the galley had the deficiencies of its merits. Its low freeboard and length made it a poor sea vessel, for it is obvious that such a long hull demanded a wide arc for turning. It could only be effectively used in comparatively calm weather. It was strictly a coastwise vessel, and although long voyages in the open sea were sometimes engaged in, such was not the usual course of its employment. When the advance of naval science and the use of firearms changed all the canons of naval warfare, the galleys still lingered for a time, useful as the scouts or eyes of the fleet. But soon the further improvement of hulls, sails, and rigging robbed them of even this function, and their last principal employment was almost as ignoble as their early career had been glorious. They were used chiefly as the means of providing a safe repository for criminals where the physical powers of these unfortunate creatures could, through their labours at the oars, be turned to the advantage of the State.

An Egyptian Galley

AN EGYPTIAN GALLEY
1600 B. C.

THE Nile region has always been a land of romance. Its antiquity and mystery fired the imagination of the Greeks and Romans. Successive later generations have acknowledged its thrall. The systematic scientific research of modern times with its discovery of the key to the riddle of the hieroglyphic writings has lifted the veil and permitted us to catch glimpses of the wonderful civilization and accomplishment of those far days, but has dispelled none of their romance.

On the walls of the temple of Deir el Bahari near Thebes are sculptured whole fleets of ships. In the illustration we see one of the vessels sent by famous Queen Hatshepsut of the 18th dynasty, to the Land of Punt. The exact location of this elusive country has not yet been determined by the Egyptologists. The name was probably generic, conveying the meaning of *a far-off land,* sometimes signifying one place, sometimes another.

Nothing can be more graphic than these temple pictures with their accompanying text. Note how similar to the Venetian gondola is the prow or stem, how graceful the stern terminating in a lotus decoration. The ship, clincher-built of cedar wood and probably about sixty-five feet long, was strengthened by a hog truss formed of wooden crotches supporting an immensely strong cable. This effectively prevented the hull from sagging or straining in a sea-way, particularly when heavily laden, because these vessels evidently were cargo carriers. The mast was probably provided with a tabernacle, so that when the yard was down, it could be lowered to offer less resistance to a contrary wind. The upper yard was fashioned of two arms or antennæ lashed together, a method persisting in certain Mediterranean types of sailing vessels until to-day. The lower yard acted as an extension for the tacks of the sail and was useful in holding down the foot. Parrels[1] confined the yards to the mast. The upper yard had its braces, and the ropes attached to the outer end of the lower yard acted as sheets. Lifts sustained both yards; when hoisted the upper yard was suspended from two, and when lowered, several sub-parts held it up, similar to the lower yard. These upper yard lifts show in the drawing in graceful curves. At the masthead an arrangement of cleats and battens furnish the means of leading the halyards, running and standing lifts for both yards.

Halyards hoisted and sustained the yard at the masthead and probably served also as backstays. In furling sail, the upper yard was let down. No forestays are shown in these relief delineations but they were certainly in use, as they appear in the Mehenkwetre models now in the Cairo Museum and Metropolitan Museum of Art at New York.

The rudder is shown on the starboard side. Perhaps there were two rudders, a very common practice. Largely em-

[1]See Note I, Appendix.

ployed in the shallow waters of the Nile, it was of prime importance that the rudder should be adjustable to the depth of the water. The rudder post was quite long, sufficiently so to enable the tiller to be rigged vertically downward. The lower part of the post was confined to the counter by a stout rope through holes pierced in the gunwales and the upper part held by a similarly arranged loose lashing to a socket or crotch at the top of a stout post, while still farther up the tiller entered it and was rotated vertically. Ropes were made fast just above the blade or loom of the rudder and belayed inboard. By this means the whole rudder could be lowered or raised as occasion demanded. These details appear fully in the Mehenkwetre models. In experiments recently made by Mr. H. E. Winlock, of the Metropolitan Museum of Art, who was one of the discoverers of these models, every rope connected with this rudder rigging was found to have its purpose, the strains nicely calculated and so arranged that practically all tension was taken from the rudder post when the boat was under way.

The form of these boats with their long overhang fore and aft was admirably adapted for landing in shoal water, necessitated by the river navigation in which they were principally engaged.

The success of the Punt expedition proves how capable were the naval architects who planned these vessels of more than thirty centuries ago, how skilful were the workmen who constructed and the mariners who manned them.

Upon the return of the ships to Thebes, laden with precious woods, incense, resin, gold, silver, and ivory, furs, live animals, and slaves, as temple-wall writings tell us, it is not to be wondered that all the people chanted hymns of praise to the power and magnificence of their heaven-born queen and to the supreme majesty of Amon-Ra, Lord High God of the terrestrial thrones!

A Greek Galley

A GREEK GALLEY
500 B. C.

NEARLY everyone will admit that among the sculptured productions of antiquity none are more satisfying in beauty, in sentiment, and in romantic interest than those from Greece.

Many of the older Greek works were produced so long ago that it almost seems as if they might have been part and parcel of the legends and myths that have come down to us from those remote times. And although they are lacking in the technical excellence attained in later Greek works of art they still show qualities of beauty and romance in embryo, especially in their association with the romantic characters that many of them portray.

Among those legends one of the most appealing is that of "Jason and the Golden Fleece." What a pity it is that the wonderful figurehead of Jason's vessel, the *Argo,* could not have been preserved. You will recall that it represented Pallas Athene and was carved from a branch of the Talking Oak of Dordona by some precursor of Praxiteles and Phidias.

Let us assume that it might have been petrified by the Medusa's head she carried on her shield. Still endowed with the all-pervading power of speech of her divine parent (for all things are possible to the gods, and what is more common than a speaking likeness, be it on canvas or in stone?) the goddess might have told us poor mortals of an age far removed from those golden days, and of the vessel over whose destinies she ruled.

Instead of being compelled to rely on ancient vase paintings, distorted by the conventions of the decorator's art, on minute seals, and on descriptions composed by authors untutored in the technique of naval affairs, she might have described to us at first hand the form of the *Argo,* her rig, the details of her construction, her decorations, and given us other information, now sadly lacking.

We can form some idea of the size of the *Argo,* because you will remember Jason summoned fifty Greek heroes to man her oars.

Assuming one hero (and they were all mighty men) to an oar, a length, according to other credible standards of comparison of about one hundred and twenty-five feet might be inferred: not so bad, for, oh, so many centuries B. C!

And then she might have told us something about Medea and Jason (for even goddesses are not above gossip) and how she had to chaperon them on the voyage back to Colchis. Perhaps she was a little jealous of Medea; and so would any one be who did not have an enchantress for either wife or sweetheart.

A Roman Trireme

A ROMAN TRIREME

MONSIEUR JAL had the satisfaction of visualizing his idea of the appearance of the ancient Roman galley. The French Government, of which Napoleon III was then the head, authorized the construction of a trireme at Clichy, one of the districts of Paris, on the Seine. The plans were drawn under the direction of the Ministry of the Marine of which M. Jal was the historiographer and the decorations were designed under the supervision of an eminent classic antiquarian. Skilled ship carpenters from one of the French naval depots were entrusted with the actual work of construction. The launching took place on March 9, 1861, in the presence of the Emperor and a distinguished company. The vessel thus produced was about 130 feet long, 17 feet broad, and 10 feet deep. Two rows of oars were stated to have been arranged upon two superposed decks with one row between the two decks.

From woodcuts appearing in the contemporary English illustrated newspapers[1] from drawings made by artists on the spot, it would seem as if Jal's theories appear to better advantage in print than in a concrete example.

Firstly, there is no evidence of the apostis, a fundamental part of the galley.

[1]*Illustrated London News,* March 21, 1861; *Illustrated London Times,* March 22, 1861.

Secondly, Jal asserted in his "Archéologie Navale," published in the year 1840, that he could admit that oars could be successfully operated from two superposed decks or stages but not from three. This he reiterates in his "Glossaire Nautique" (1848–50). And yet the cuts show three superposed rows of oars and the text accompanying the said illustrations confirms this arrangement.

It is a little difficult to understand how M. Jal managed two superposed decks or stages in this narrow vessel, one having a ratio of length to breadth of nearly seven and a half to one. Such a craft would necessarily have more draught than would a wider one. It is hardly probable that it drew less than four feet of water. In such a vessel the lowest row of oar holes must necessarily have been located at a point high enough above the water line to prevent a moderately rough sea from entering these openings pierced in the ship's side. Moreover, it would have been imperative to obtain freedom from wave interference in the manipulation of the oars. In a vessel of the size above described, one which would not ride easily over the waves like a wider boat, such a point could scarcely have been less than four feet above the water. Taking into consideration the above figures, and estimating the head-room of the lowest stage to be a minimum of four and one half feet, it will be seen that the upper deck or stage would be about even with the top of the bulwarks, leaving no place for the support of the fulcrum for the highest row of oars.

Thirdly, as regards the intermediate row of oars, one must assume that the oarsmen of this row were seated on benches or stages nearer the medial axis of the vessel, that the inboard portion of their oars was longer in proportion to the lower and upper rows, and that the oar openings were arranged in lines inclined from the perpendicular so that the rowers did not interfere with one another.

Fourthly, M. Jal seems to have rejected entirely in his concrete example the assertion contained in his "Archéologie Navale," Mémoire No. 4, that the arrangement of the oars in triremes, quadremes, penteremes, etc., of the ancient Greeks and Romans was in effect the system called *à zenzile* and employed in the Mediterranean galleys as late as the 15th Century. The galleys using it were propelled by groups of three or more oarsmen all sitting upon the same bench, each rower pulling a separate oar. The benches were not set exactly at right angles to the keel, the inside end being slightly farther out and higher than the outer end. This arrangement accords perfectly with the evidence alluded to in our introduction as embodied in the apostis shown on the Winged Victory of Samothrace.

M. Jal has, in his said Mémoire No. 4, given a number of illustrations from both classical and Renaissance sources, showing this arrangement *à zenzile*. He discusses the system at considerable length and gives several diagrams to scale to demonstrate the possibility of its application to as many as six oars in a group. It is rather strange that he did not follow this method in his galley of the year 1861.

Our illustration shows what we believe is a rational view of a trireme of classical times. The apostis furnished support for the rowing benches and uniform width for the leverage of the oars extended well over the galley's side. The advantage of having all the groups of oars exert their effort in substantially the same line is obvious.

In the appendix will be found a diagram giving a view of the disposition of the oars of a galley so arranged with oars in groups of three.

The Viking Long Ship

THE VIKING LONG SHIP

SNORRI said, "Harold, seest thou this long ship? It is much like the Dragon which King Olaf Tryggvason (995-1000 A. D.) had built at Hladhamrar after the model of Raud's serpent. He brought that vessel from Halogaland. The stocks were very long and the ship's keel measured over 65 ells. Thorberg Shafhogg was the stem-smith. While the bulwarks were rising, Thorberg had to go back to his farm. He was gone a long time, and when he returned the bulwarks were completed. The same evening the King and Thorberg went to see how the ship looked. Everybody praised it. The King then went back to his house. Early next morning the King and Thorberg went down to see the ship again. All the smiths had arrived and stood there doing no work. 'Are you on a strike?' asked the King. They said 'No, but someone has spoiled the ship.' Notches had been cut into the gunwale on one side from stem to stern. The King was furious and swore that if he could find out who had ruined the ship from envy, that man should die, but he who could name the doer of the deed should get great reward. Thorberg said, 'I can tell you, O King, who did this deed.' The King answered, 'Thou, O Thorberg, wast the likeliest man to be so lucky as to ascertain this thing and to tell me.' 'I will tell the King who has done it,' he said. 'I have done it,'

'What,' said the King, amazed, 'thou?' 'Yes, I,' said Thorberg. The King answered, 'Thou shalt repair it so that it is as good as it was before, or thou shalt lose thy life.' Thorberg shaped the gunwale so that all the cuts disappeared. The King and everybody said that the ship was much better on the side which Thorberg had shaped. Then the King asked Thorberg to do the same thing to the other side of the ship and thanked him well for it. Thereafter, Thorberg was chief smith of the ship until it was finished. Its beak and dragon tail were all ornamented with gold. Its gunwales were as high as those of seagoing ships. No better or costlier vessel had ever been built in Norway."[1]

Thanks to the blue clay of the Scandinavian hills which has preserved several examples almost intact, we know exactly how these vessels looked. The story of the finding of the Gogstadt ship is quite as romantic as any treasure-trove tale by Poe or Stevenson, and it is fact, not fiction.

The size of the ancient Norse vessels was determined by the number of "rooms" (*rums*) or rowing benches. King Olaf's ship, the saga says, contained thirty rooms. If the ship was 65 ells or 135 feet on the flat of the keel, it would probably have an additional length fore and aft of fifteen feet respectively for the curving rise of the stem and stern or a total length of 165 feet. Allowing four feet for each room, or 120 feet, this would leave 45 feet for purposes of forward and after decks and space free from the rowing benches.

---

[1]See Olaf Tryggvason's Saga, c 79, for account of the construction of a Viking ship of this date.

The sailing equipment of these ships was rather rudimentary. Primarily intended to be propelled by oars, their floors were rather flat with very easy lines of entrance and departure. The sides rose almost vertically with quite a sharp turn in the bilge. With a free wind they must have sailed fast. Any one who has had the experience of sailing in a rowing boat of fine lines, such as the St. Lawrence skiff, will appreciate this fact. The mast had an elaborate step, something like a double fish tail, into the forward opening of which the foot of the mast fitted into a step-hold. It was wedged or keyed into its upright position by a stout oak plank, somewhat resembling in shape an old-fashioned boot-jack. Stays fore and aft and shrouds on the side supported the mast after it had been raised into its vertical position from the crotches placed aft to support it when horizontal.

When recumbent, the mast served as a part of the ridge-pole of the tent which at night covered the whole vessel, the sides of the tent being fastened along the gunwales. The yard was hoisted by a tie passing through a hole in a mast head and was held close to the mast by a wooden cleat or parrel. Braces and sheets led aft, and tacks of the sail were sometimes extended by the light booms. Cleats were provided for the purpose of belaying the several ropes.

The rudder was always rigged up the right side, hence the derivation of our word "starboard" from *stjorbordi*, "steering side," while the left side, *backbordi*, may be traced through the Normans in the French word *bâbord*, port.

On the starboard quarter of the vessel a large rounded oak boss was firmly bolted to the outside, the extreme outer surface of which was in a line perpendicular to the gunwale. Through the gunwale, slightly forward of this perpendicular line, two holes were pierced to receive the grommet, a rope passing out one hole, around the rudder post, and then in again through the other hole, belaying inside. A large hole was bored through the upper part of the rudder blade and also through the above described boss and the ship's side. Through this passed a heavy rope knotted at the outer end and terminating inside the ship where it made fast; this served as the axis of the rudder. An iron ring fastened to the after edge of the rudder blade to which was attached a cord leading on deck provided the means, when the grommet was slacked off, by which the rudder could be raised or lowered on its aforesaid axis. A square hole in the upper part of the rudder-post served to receive a transverse tiller. This the steersman sat behind and pushed or pulled, as he desired, to direct the vessel's course. The oars had narrow pointed blades and were thrust through holes pierced in the sides. When the oars were withdrawn, these oar-ports were closed by circular shutters fastened upon the inside. Large ships had several anchors. Merchant ships, the seagoing vessels referred to above, had a single permanent mast and few oars or none. They were heavier, shorter, and had higher sides.

How fine these war vessels or "dragons" must have looked with their golden figureheads, tails, and weather vanes. Their sides were usually painted in red, purple, and golden stripes, the shields of their warriors, usually of two contrasting colours with gleaming metal rims and bosses hanging crescentwise along the gunwales, while the sails of different coloured cloth, often embroidered, and some even of two-piled velvet, swelled aloft.

The gaily painted oar-blades rose and fell rhythmically amid cascades of sun-lit jewelled drops, as the vessels dipped and swayed in the heaving waters of the fjords, against a background of dark beetling cliffs and deep coloured evergreens. Good ships, stout warriors, brave seamen.

The Seventeenth Century Galley

THE SEVENTEENTH CENTURY GALLEY

PROBABLY little change was manifest in the appearance of the galley during the latter centuries of its existence. It was one of those types whose permanence was the result of an early arrival at full efficiency. When cannon were introduced, some modification of the galley's upper structure was demanded for their installation.

The illustration shows the low narrow vessel with the beak, the apostis, and the elaborate stern elongated by the extension of the after gunwales to a considerable distance beyond the narrow transom, if such a peculiar form of construction can claim that name.

The after deck was covered by a structure the upper part of which was sometimes shaped like the ceiling of a barrel vaulted room. This, called the "carosse," served as the Captain's quarters.

Ordinarily, the galleys of this period were equipped with two masts, the one nearest the bow being usually the larger. The long lateen yards were composed of two members called antennæ, the thicker parts of which were lashed together in the middle to form a single spar—a very ancient form of construction.

The masts were supported by shrouds usually set up with blocks instead of deadeyes. The gear for hoisting the yards will be fully described hereafter. Double guys held down the yard and kept it in place toward the foot of the mast, while other tackle, probably similar to the mizzen bowlines, fitted to the lateen mizzens of the round ships, hauled the heel of the yard to one side or other, as occasion demanded. Vangs controlled the after part of the yard, while brails caught up the sail to the yard for furling.

Some of the older galleys were fitted with three rudders, one at the stern and one on each quarter.

The rowers' benches were distributed along the sides within the apostis to starboard and port, leaving between them a gangway extending lengthwise called the "coursier." Just in front of the carosse was a balcony extending athwartship with small stages outboard on each side whence ladders gave access to the vessel. Below the carosse was another chamber called the "gavon" lighted by narrow rectangular openings in the vessel's sides, protected by sliding shutters. This form of window was a feature of many old-time vessels. A sort of raised forecastle, well forward, furnished to the sailors a space removed both from the rowers and gunners in which to work the foresail.

The galleys of this period were superbly decorated with gilded bas-reliefs and mouldings. Their flags, streamers, and banners were often made of silk embroidered with gold and coloured threads. The carosse was not infrequently covered with a "tendelet'" of crimson silk damask. What a gallant spectacle such a vessel must have presented as with oars held high, lateen sails swelling, with silken flags fluttering, it swept along over the sparkling waters of the azure midland sea!

The Galleass

THE GALLEASS

J<small>AL</small> says that this name (*galeasse* in old French) was the name given first to a galley larger and stronger than the common galley, but resembling it closely. This large galley or galleass, as it was called in English, had been considerably developed by the end of the 15th Century. During the middle of the 16th Century, vessels of this form played an important rôle in all great naval combats. They were the deciding factors in the battle of Lepanto (1571), resulting in the victory of the western nations in their struggle against the menace of Turkish domination in Europe. They also fought valiantly on both sides in what Jal calls the fatal "*rencontre*" between the Spanish and English, ending in the destruction of the Invincible Armada in 1588.

Pantero-Pantaro writing in 1614, describing the Venetian galleass of the period, says that such a vessel of twenty-five or more oars on a side, compared with an ordinary galley, would be about a third longer, and wide and high in proportion. Forward and aft it had large platforms or decks upon which stood a part of its broadside artillery. This part of the vessel also served as a vantage point for the soldiery.

A solid deck covered the waist above the rowers and afforded also a large open space for handling the sails, and upon which a considerable number of guns and soldiers could be placed.

Less swift than the ordinary galley, its usual place was in the second line of the advance guard of the battle, and it was in this position that the largest galleasses of the Armada were placed. And it was from such a vessel that the Duc de Medina Sydonia, who commanded that great gathering of vessels of war, conducted his operations.

The Mediterranean galleass was usually lateen rigged with all the peculiarities of that style obtaining in the galley.

In England during the reign of Henry VIII the word "galleass" seems to have been applied to several types of vessels, but by the end of the 16th Century the term was generally confined to a form of large ship with high freeboard propelled by oars either with or without sail power. John Montgomery, in a treatise entitled "Concerning the Navie of England" (1570–1588), says that "Galliasses brook the seas as well as others," and that "Shipes to saile and row have advantages over others." He says that a galleass of six hundred tons and having twenty oars on a side would require five men at each oar.

While one of the outstanding and persisting features of the galley was its far-projecting beak-head or ram, it does not seem that this spur was ever a marked characteristic of the galleass. It is true that representations of the vessel are found embodying this feature, but that it was of little use for ramming in a vessel of the type we are considering must soon have become apparent.

This form of beak-head ultimately changed to the form

in which we see it in the illustration depicting a galleass of the middle of the 17th Century, and it is in this form that we find it in most of the sailing ships of that period.

The Turkish mahona seems to have been, during the 17th Century, about the equivalent of the Venetian galleass of that time. And probably the respective Christian and Mussulman vessels of a century earlier were quite similar in form and size.

If any one wishes to learn in detail the part that the galleass played in saving western Europe from Turkish invasion, he may find it graphically set forth in the late Commodore F. A. Parker's description of the Battle of Lepanto in his "Fleets of the World, The Galley Period."

PART II
ROUND SHIPS

ROUND SHIPS

It has been seen that the proportion of breadth to length was greater in the round ships than in the galleys.

The long ships of early times were primarily the vessels of war, celerity of movement being of the utmost importance. The round ships, both of antiquity and of the Middle Ages, constructed to carry heavy cargoes, were not exactly swift movers. Not that the round ships of these times were not sometimes used for fighting: quite the reverse. Although usually designed as carriers of freight and passengers, their greater bulk naturally enabled them to embark a greater number of armed men, and later, when cannon were introduced, to mount armaments disposed in a manner impossible in the long narrow rowing craft, where the chief points of vantage for placing guns of large calibre, i.e., low down amidship, were preëmpted by the benches and oars of the rowers. Adaptability for fighting was, in still later times, further advanced by their ever-increasing mobility, a quality in which eventually, excepting in a calm, they surpassed the long ship.

Until practically the end of the 18th Century, quite large vessels, such as ship-rigged sloops of war and small frigates, as well as brigs, brigantines, and schooners, were often equipped with oars.

By a curious verbal transposition the square sails of the round ships were sometimes called in certain maritime localities round sails; while the ships themselves on account of the shape of their rectangular canvas were designated as square ships.

By far the greater number of vessels described in this work have been grouped under the class of round ships.

And yet many known types have been omitted, especially those bearing what are known as fore and aft rigs. When they have been shown it has been because in some manner their equipment included, albeit only incidentally, some feature of the square rig.

There has seemed to the authors a modernity in the fore and aft rig (although it has a clear title to considerable antiquity), a modernness emphasized by its very persistence and universality in the face of the gradual late disappearance of so many of the old-time square riggers; this has been the deciding factor in excluding it from this collection. For like old friends and old wives, we middle-aged folk (and probably many of the younger ones, too) like the old square-rigged ships best.

A Greek Merchantman

A GREEK MERCHANTMAN

PHILOCROTES, the Athenian merchant, gazed at the busy scene about him. Timon, the Corinthian ship master, stood beside him, his keen eyes taking in the smallest detail of the work going on under his command. A vessel hauled out for repairs was about to be set again into the water for a trading voyage to the Cyclades.

"O, my son," said the merchant, "have the specifications reported to me by the shipwrights been faithfully performed?" "Yes, master," replied Timon, "but the report of the foreman carpenter seemed to me faulty in that he would replace the broken planking with plain deals instead of cedar wood. I therefore compelled him to substitute the latter. This he did grudgingly, saying that thereby he would lose all his profit." "Therein thou hast done well, my son, and to my interest. And hast thou seen that such of the bronze plates below the oar holes as were broken have been renewed? That the new cotton cloth for the sail is of full weight and free from flaws? And that the arsenic and sulphur have been well mixed with the Chian oil thou broughtest back on thy last voyage and the mixture evenly applied to the vessel's sides that she may speed through the blue waters freely and without impediment?" To all these rapid questions the young man nodded his assent.

His employer continued, "And hast thou seen to it also that the careless wielders of the brush have not damaged the beautiful ship's eyes that I had placed upon her forward sides by Andimion, the skilful Persian slave of my friend Araxes?" "Verily, master, thou shouldst know that I would permit naught to harm them, otherwise how would my darling see the rocks and shoals and know how to avoid them on the dark nights when Notos blows and we have naught else to guide us but the light of the stars?

"And another thing have I done. Recallest thou the bundle of staves I brought back from Tyre? I had them from a Phœnician trader who told me they had been brought from the very far-off west. Thou saidst then, a little peevishly, that I did thereby waste thy money, but soon forgot thy irritation. I have had them fashioned into oars, and never were there lighter or stronger ones. Try, master, if thou canst, by bending all thy weight on it, break one." The older man examined the oar carefully and nodded approval. "In this also hast thou done excellently well, my son. Ever thou doest as well for my interest as I would for myself. May the Gods preserve and bless thee. Look to it also, for my and thy sake, that all the cords be strong and the wattles along the topsides well plaited and tough, for there will be perishable goods aboard, that must be kept from the waves and spray."

"And now come with me, O Timon, to the pleasant shade of Eubotes' wine shop that we may drain together a cup of his best Lesbian and decide upon that with which we shall lade thy bark."[1]

[1] See Note 2, Appendix.

The Roman Corbita or Merchantman

THE ROMAN CORBITA OR MERCHANTMAN

THE steady increase in the foreign affairs of Rome, both military and civil, necessitated proportionate augmentations of both her navy and merchant marine.

Increasingly large importations of all sorts of commodities demanded more and larger carriers. The great corn fleets from the granaries of the Near East and Africa maintained a continuous course across the inland sea, while the transports required to furnish supplies to her numerous armies engaged in conquest in various parts of the then known world, as well as the means of conveying the troops themselves, must have reached numerical proportions not very different from those obtaining many centuries later.

The Romans imported all sorts of objects of art into Italy from conquered lands. Some of these articles were of large size and great weight. And while it is possible that specially designed barges may have been constructed to carry such ponderous objects as the obelisks brought from Egypt, yet it is not at all improbable that many pieces of colossal statuary were transported in the larger merchant round ship. These vessels seem to have reached generous proportions. For the marine architects of a civilization which could produce so large a floating structure as the imperial pleasure boat, the remains of which have been examined and measured under the waters of Lake Nemi, would not balk at the construction of sea-going vessels of at least a thousand tons burden.

It seems remarkable that, considering the tens of thousands of vessels produced during the long period of Rome's great marine activity, not one has been wholly preserved for us by some chance such as that which saved the Gokstad ship from decay and that so few graphic representations of these ships remain to us out of the great number of more or less perfect monuments of Roman greatness.

A number of ancient coins and medals show us vessels, but in these, as in more modern cases, the artist was limited by the scope of his field, and such representations are always conventionalized. Other representations are scarcely more satisfactory.

The accompanying illustration shows a rationalized version of a Roman merchant ship adapted from a monument discovered at Ostium, the great ancient seaport of Rome. The original sculpture, if reliable (and it is believed to be so), shows most of the exterior details of hull and rigging of a merchant ship of that period. These merchant vessels of the larger sort were called corbitæ, from *corbis,* a basket, thus named because they carried such a receptacle at their mastheads in order to indicate their occupation as carriers of both passengers and merchandise. It is said that these Roman merchantmen were of heavy construction and were noted for their slow sailing.

The sheer of the ship was considerable, and the rotundity of the fabric served as a pattern for the round ships of a thousand years later. The high swelling stern was admirably adapted to minimize the effect of following seas—a constant source of menace to ships proceeding principally before the wind. The form of the wales probably is predicted upon and indicative of some features of internal construction, but as to this we cannot be certain.

No exception can be taken to the form of shrouds set up by deadeyes and lanyards, nor to the manner of tightening the prominent stays. The curious topsail composed of triangular halves has survived to our own day and generation. Attention may likewise be directed to the form of brails, the ropes passing through rings sewed upon the sail in rows perpendicular to the yard. This device effectively confined the folds of the sails. Although if the canvas was heavy a sail so brailed must have been bulky and somewhat difficult to furl properly.

The bowsprit was then no innovation, but its use seems to have been practically disregarded, if not forgotten, during the Dark Ages. Taken altogether it may be safely assumed that this vessel was wholly adequate to the demands made upon it and that its minor appliances and internal arrangements of which we are unfortunately totally ignorant were the result of an evolution, as sure and as practical as that of our modern vessels.

The form of this old ship is the embodiment of grace, and its ornamentation lends to it a dignity compatible with that of the then Mistress of the World.

Among the late discoveries at Ostium is a fresco showing a Roman merchant vessel in the process of lading.

Five personages in all appear upon the ship's deck, while

two more carry sacks, presumably of grain, up a gang plank. The central and most important figure is labelled *Arascantus*, probably the owner. Standing aft on the raised deck of the cabin and holding the tiller of one of the rudders (for two are shown) is another man, labelled *Farnaces, Magister*, evidently the captain.

In form, this painting of a ship resembles closely our illustration. A bare mast appears without rigging or sail.

Little by little more facts are continually coming to light showing the development of the vessels of early times and gradually filling the gaps in the order of their evolution. Let us hope that in the not too distant future the line will be complete.

A Mediæval Ship

A MEDIÆVAL SHIP

It is indeed little we know of the ships of that dark period between the fall of the Roman power and the first re-awakenings of pictorial art. We have only a single intermediate concrete example—the Gokstad ship, heretofore described. That there were seagoing ships at this time we know from the sagas; also from the monkish manuscripts, the minstrel lays, the folk stories and fables.

We may believe that for many centuries, at the beginning of our era, there was little or no change in the craft that sailed the seas or closely skirted the shores. So to picture a ship of the Dark Ages is to draw upon our imagination, limiting our vision by the horizon of our scanty knowledge.

Therefore, be lenient, we pray thee, with our day-dream, for it is naught but romance in both senses of the word.

Nor can we do better than to quote a scene of shipping from that fantastically appealing and altogether delightful fairy tale of William Morris, entitled "The Wood Beyond the World."

"He saw there a tall ship . . . a ship all boun, which had her boats out, and men sitting to the oars thereof ready to tow her outwards when the hawser should be cast off, and by seeming her mariners were but abiding for some one or other to come aboard.

"So Walter stood idly watching the said ship and as he looked, lo! folk passing him toward the gangway. These were three; first came a dwarf, dark-brown of hue and hideous . . . After him came a maiden, young by seeming . . . fair of face as a flower, gray-eyed, brown-haired, with lips full and red, slim and gentle of body. Simple was her array, of a short and strait green gown, so that on her right ankle was clear to see an iron ring. . . . Last of the three was a lady, tall and stately, so radiant of visage and glorious of raiment that it was hard to say what like she was . . .

"They went over the gangway into the ship . . . then he saw how the hawser was cast off and the boats fell to tugging the big ship towards the harbour-mouth with hale and how of men. Then the sail fell down from the yard and was sheeted home and filled with the fair wind as the ship's bows ran up on the first green wave outside the haven. Even therewith the shipmen cast abroad a banner, whereon was done in a green field a grim wolf ramping up against a maiden, and so went the ship upon her way."

A Thirteenth Century English Warship

A THIRTEENTH CENTURY ENGLISH WARSHIP

No CONCRETE example of a north European ship of this period is known to have been preserved as have several Scandinavian vessels of a few hundred years earlier. Obviously the chances of the preservation of such a craft are all against us. Christianity gradually banished the pagan rites which surrounded a chieftain in his last resting place with his late earthly possessions. So archæology owes much to paganism. The date upon which to base a pictorial representation of a ship of the time of the Crusades must therefore of necessity be documentary. By this term is meant representations of ships as seen by the eyes of the early artists, whatever may be the media through which they have expressed themselves.

Fortunately some data exist to furnish us with a fair, if not perfect, idea of how the ship of the 13th Century looked.

We may judge that during two or three centuries between the making of the famous Bayeaux tapestry showing ships of the middle of the 11th Century, and the dates of the many 13th and 14th Century seals of English and French Channel ports, not much change took place in either in the form of hull or in the rigging. Such improvements as were made seem to be additions to hull in the shape of removable platforms fore and aft. These ultimately became permanent parts of the ship's structure.

But if we cannot with conviction say that we are wholly satisfied with such facts as we possess about these ships, it is our privilege on the other hand to supply from our imagination any attributes with which we may wish to endow them, conformably with other facts applicable to this romantic age.

Let us weave around them romances of voyages to the Holy Land, of encounters with strange and unbelievably greater ships of the land-locked central sea, and with pirates in swift-sailing craft along the north African coast.

Let us people their waists with men-at-arms in leather jerkins, the after castle with knights in armour, and the forecastle with archers and seamen. The military top, square or round, bristles with darts while the crane hoists up molten lead, stones, and fire-brands to cast down on decks of the enemy.

Or suppose that a princess goes by sea to join her future princely husband. The ship is bedecked with fair golden sail and the cloths about the bulwarks bear the lady's colours. The pavese (row of shields) about the sides is bright with the arms of the two families about to be joined together. The lady and her maidens work with their needles or bobbins on the after castle under a gaily striped awning, or pace softly along the deck in the shade of the huge billowing sail, while a minstrel chants his master's praise or beguiles the tedium of the voyage with recitations such as the Roman de la Rose, the Lai du Petit Oiselet, and the Chanson de Roland.

An Early Fifteenth Century Merchant Ship

AN EARLY FIFTEENTH CENTURY
MERCHANT SHIP

THE science of ship-building had made a very considerable advance by the middle of the 15th Century. Not only
were there ships of large tonnage, but those carrying four
masts were not uncommon. Evidently two-masted ships were
also to be met with. But if manuscripts and missals of
the period are to be relied upon, some larger vessels clung
to the old-fashioned style of a single mast. The difficulty
with this testimony is that many such documents were often
merely copies of earlier illuminations, and so cannot be relied upon as contemporary renderings of the ships of such
later date.

An engraver of this period who signs with the initials
"I. M." (Israel von Mekenem), working somewhat in the
style of the famous artist signing himself "W. A.," who en-
graved both the details of the rigging and hulls of the vessels
he depicted with most meticulous care, has given us a print
showing such a two-masted ship. It is interesting to note
that this vessel has no forecastle and that the bowsprit is
stepped to the right of the foremast and curiously curving
stem-head, the latter style traceable in small craft of much
later times. A curious emblem decorates the bowsprit.

The absence of the mizzenmast leaves us somewhat in

doubt as to the function of the crotch at the taffrail unless it may be assumed that the main mast can be lowered and supported thereby. Across the deck in the waist are curved awning supports suggesting that a deck cargo liable to be affected by the elements may have been carried. The poop deck, graced by substantial lanterns, is built upon *stanchions,* a characteristic of the period.

It is practically impossible to assign a name to this old-time vessel, but she is certainly not a ship of war. Perhaps she was a passenger ship, but if so, she does not look very comfortable. In fact, sea travel at this period was not the height of luxury. Hammocks had not yet been introduced and the voyager in such a ship as this would have been compelled to sleep on a truss of straw in a cabin hardly large enough for a dog. These ships were perpetually wet, and the odour of the bilge could hardly be compared to Coty's perfumes.

But let us hasten to overlook these aspects of the voyage and to think only of the brave adventures of the traveller and the fine yarns his sea experiences would enable him to recount to his family and friends when once he had recovered from his mal-de-mer and got rid of his sea legs.

The Carrack

THE CARRACK

THE word employed to designate the larger ships of an indeterminate period, which certainly embraced the 14th, 15th, and part of the 16th centuries, and probably a considerable period of time prior to the earlier date mentioned above, was carrack. Appearing in various forms such as carraca, carraque, and kraeck, the term is of doubtful origin. Jal rejects its derivation from Κάραβος. Mr. Nance says that the word is of Mediterranean origin, but does not state the source.

During the period above mentioned it was essentially a vessel designed to carry large burdens, but often employed also for purposes of war, and was undoubtedly an integral part of the shipping of all European maritime nations, although, as to some countries, it may not be possible to identify it by name with any particular individual ship.

The carrack differed from the nef in that it was bigger, of greater draught, and had higher top-sides. Some were probably as large as one thousand tons.

Fortunately we have one excellent representation and several other tolerable ones upon which to found our illustration. It must be continually borne in mind that the forms of hull and rigging of the carracks, as well as of practically all other vessels, at any given date would be found to have differed somewhat in each different locality and that changes were constantly taking place from time to time in such forms in each of such places. So that the best we can do is to say that our illustration shows a Northern carrack taken from a print of the engraver who signed himself with a mark that looks somewhat like the letters W. A. The date may be placed about the middle of the 15th Century. The print referred to, which has the sovereign merit of giving the name of the vessel represented, while offering all one could reasonably expect from an artist of this period, is not by any means perfect.

It is only by supplying its defects from other sources that one can arrive at a reasonable representation of the whole.

It will be seen that the carrack usually had four large wales. Skids strengthened the sides. In the carracks of Southern waters it was customary to permit the ends of the deck beams to project beyond the planking of the vessel's sides. These ships usually had three, sometimes four, masts, the mainmast being much larger than the other two. A diminutive main-topmast appeared at quite an early date, but this spar was often little more than a flag-staff.

One of the most recent "finds" showing representations of carracks is an illustration to a French translation of Boccaccio's "La Teseide." It is in the Vienna National Library. Usually such miniature illustrations of contemporary 15th Century books and manuscripts, owing to their small scale and conventional handlings, are of little value in furnishing reliable information as to the shipping of this period.

The picture above referred to is a happy exception. It offers many points of confirmation to other drawings, prints, and paintings. Mr. Nance has given an interesting review of the subject of carracks, and particularly of the sources from which the information concerning them is drawn, in the *Mariner's Mirror,* vol. IX, no. 5, May, 1923.

He there describes the Boccaccio drawing and compares it with other representations of carracks, giving references to earlier articles upon the same subject, in that magazine. The search for information upon these matters is one of the latter-day romances of the old ship. It is a fascinating study in which the opportunity for original work is unlimited.

Late Fifteenth Century Ship

LATE FIFTEENTH CENTURY SHIP

LIKE nearly all other branches of archæological research, the branch dealing with the ship has, within the last fifteen years, made very definite advances.

Much that the indefatigable efforts of M. Jal were not able to discover is gradually coming to light. While interesting, the task of the modern searchers after the facts of mediæval and renaissance naval architecture is arduous. It demands the examination of numberless time-stained parchments, of crumbling papers, of ancient volumes stowed in out-of-the-way corners of libraries, and of musty records in remote naval and marine repositories. But the searchers are constantly adding to the store of information upon the subject.

The highest praise is not too much to bestow upon the painstaking specialists contributing to the pages of the *Mariner's Mirror,* the periodical published by the British Society for Nautical Research.

It is unfortunate that the well-meaning Spanish gentleman who prepared the plans and designs for the Columbus fleet sent to the United States for the Chicago Celebration in the year 1892 could not have had the benefit of the effort of these English scientists. It is safe to say that if he had, the alleged replica of the *Santa Maria*, the principal result of his earnest if misdirected efforts, would not have borne the form she does—for she is still in existence, disseminating to this day a deplorable amount of misinformation; while models fashioned after her, based upon the same erroneous data, are legion and may be seen even in such repositories as the Science Museum at South Kensington in London and the Smithsonian Institution at Washington, D. C.

It is also curious that one of the Italian Government's literary contributions to the Columbian celebration, a superbly printed treatise on the subject of naval architecture in the time of Christopher Columbus, its pages filled with illustrations giving much of the information if not the complete appearance of a ship of the latter part of the 15th Century, should have adopted the said rendering of the *Nao Santa Maria,* as the final estimate of the evidence so presented.

The round ship of that date was round and no mistake. As Mr. R. Norton Nance humorously says of the carracks of that time, "The compass seems to have decided the form, not only of the stem, but also of the mid-ship sections." The curves of the sheer are almost equally generous. Prominent wales and skids formed part of the exterior structure.

In addition to rotundity, giving that certain appearance of bulk that all generously curved bodies possess, the next conspicuous feature was the great size and height of the mainmast. It is the apotheosis of the mast-tree of the once single-masted vessel, assisted now in a very small way, not supplemented, by two, sometimes by three, young sprouts of masts, small saplings still, but destined in time to grow into formidable rivals but never quite compeers. The square mainsail, too, was still out of all proportion to the other sails, probably embracing twice the area of the balance of the ship's canvas put together.

It is highly improbable that the original *Santa Maria* had a square tuck such as has been given her by her modern Spanish reproducer, or that her fore and after castles resembled in any wise the early 17th Century forms exhibited in what he would have us believe is "an exact counterpart" of the Genoese navigator's vessel. The arrangement and sheer of the decks were quite different also. Nor is it believable that at this date the transom could have conceivably been of a form permitting the display of a large and nearly rectangular painting of the Holy Virgin, no matter how appropriate and desirable such a talisman might be.

Speaking of the talisman, it was quite customary at this date for a harbinger of good fortune in the form of a bullock's horns to be installed upon the end of the bowsprit or for a goat's skull to grace the extremity of this spar.

The late 15th Century ships sometimes carried a small topmast bearing an almost microscopic topsail sheeted into the top. In the modern *Santa Maria's* rigging the topsail is quite large and the sheets lead to the arms of the main yard.

In other matters of rigging, particularly in a ship of a southern European country, the main stay would have been set up to the stem-head with a lanyard in connection with an elaborate collar device as yet not clearly explained; the shrouds would have been galley fashion, that is, without ratlines, and access to the main top would have been gained by means of a Jacob's ladder aft of the mast.

Lifts and bowlines would be present, while the braces would be of a much more rudimentary form than in the new

Santa Maria's equipment. Altogether this later production both in hull and in rigging resembles much more nearly a ship of the first part of the 17th Century than one of more than two hundred years earlier. It is probable that in some form, martlets and martnets, the forerunners of the leach lines and bunt lines, were then in use, with brails for the lantern mizzen similar to those employed upon the Mediterranean galleys.

Tacks and sheets would be much as we would expect to find them, while one would probably be astonished to discover, if such a vessel could be found to-day intact, how apt and convenient was most of her subordinate gear.

While to us they would seem inadequate, these late 15th Century ships, especially those of the larger size (and it is quite probable that some of them exceeded eight hundred tons), were probably not bad seagoing vessels.

Of course, they went to windward slowly or not at all. But with fair luck (of which they had at least an average) and with good management (of which they certainly had much) it is not surprising that it was in a vessel of this sort that Columbus ventured out to the westward in order to report officially to the Spanish sovereigns the existence of that land destined to play a revolutionary part in the development of the sailing ship, the land of which the reputed discoverer of the New World had heard from an unnamed but positively theretofore existent Portuguese pilot, his certain predecessor in that romantic feat.

These statements may seem iconoclastic, but they are based upon solid facts.

An Early Sixteenth Century Ship

AN EARLY SIXTEENTH CENTURY SHIP

OF ALL the sumptuous fabrics which the imagination and ingenuity of man have devised in which to wend his way in splendour across the great deep, none has surpassed in romance and magnificence the *Henri Grâce à Dieu* or *Great Harry* of the year 1514. Henry VII had in his day constructed a great ship comparing not unfavourably in size with all but the largest vessels of three hundred years later. So that the ship of Henry VIII was not large for her epoch, although she was probably of about one thousand tons burden.

That which appeals particularly to our sense of the romantic was the lavishness of her fitting-out when she was prepared to carry the King across the Channel for his meeting with François I at the Field of the Cloth of Gold.

Launched at Erith, she was already six years old when she was taken in hand for this event. It was customary for all war vessels of this time to carry along their rails rows of shields called a pavese. In the *Great Harry,* these heater shields, or targets, as they were called, were displayed even around the tops. They were placed in groups of four, decorated respectively with the following devices: viz., the cross of Saint George on a silver ground, a golden fleur-de-lys on a blue ground, the Tudor rose on a green-and-white ground, and the golden portcullis on a red ground. Furthermore, the sails were on this occasion made of cloth of gold, damasked. Long forked pennants flew gaily from the mastheads, yardarms, and other parts of the vessel, the cross of Saint George predominating. At the corners of the poop were banners bearing the Tudor dragons on a green-and-white ground, and at the similar corners of the forecastle the royal arms of England were borne on golden-tipped lances.

The vessel's high sides were covered with gothic windows and panels, artistically painted and gilded. Into these the wales and skids, the structural parts of the ship, gracefully blended. The stern, above the square tuck, rose in curving tiers, and the narrow after part of the poop was studded with gothic windows and bristled with cannon, if we can believe the contemporary painting of Vincente Volpe, depicting the King's departure from Dover harbour on May 31, 1520.

Staunch as she looked, the *Great Harry* probably was a bit cranky, as the King declined to return from France aboard her. Perhaps his overthrow in a friendly wrestling bout with the jovial Francis had something to do with his decision.

At all events, the *Great Harry* must have been a thrilling and splendid sight as she stood out of the harbour, her great golden sails swelling in the soft spring breeze, her flags and banners fluttering, the royal trumpeters, an indispensable adjunct upon such an occasion, blowing forth pæans of martial music, with the lustre of the kingly presence lending an added glamour to her almost conscious magnificence.

The illustration is intended to be a rationalized version, drawn from contemporary sources without exactly copying any particular one, of such a ship as the *Great Harry* may have been.[1]

[1] See Note 3, Appendix.

The Hulk

THE HULK

ONE of the most interesting subjects in the study of the English language is that which concerns itself with the changes wrought by time and use in the meaning of words. The point is well illustrated in "hulk." During the early years of the 16th Century it was applied to a type of the larger-size vessel. This craft was round sterned, square tucked, high pooped, covered with weak and ineffectual clench work or skids. The rig was substantially that of the ship of a corresponding date. The appearance of the more efficient Dutch flute in the course of the century seems to have marked the hulk's extinction. At the period mentioned great fleets of hulks are recorded, each ship ranging in size from one hundred to eight hundred tons. A type of vessel called a Marsillian is stated to have been the Mediterranean counterpart of the hulk.

To-day the term "hulk" signifies a vessel reduced to its poorest, meanest condition, the remains or carcass of a ship.

At its prime, the hulk constituted one of the principal classes of cargo carriers of merchant vessels *par excellence*. Maritime trade was expanding rapidly in the 16th Century, and with the increase in the size of the vessels themselves the conditions and comfort of the sailors were improving also.

It is interesting to learn of the sea-kit of a merchant sea-man in the year 1540. This is what John Griffin, a quarter-master of the *Barbara,* took with him on a voyage to Brazil: a silver whistle and chain, a ship's chest, a cape of new black frysdown, a coat of black cloth with sleeves, a doublet of blue changeable camlot, a white fustian jerkin, also one of green, a white frieze coat, with sleeves, two pairs of long hose, one green the other blue, two pairs of white hose, one pair of long white breeches, two shirts of fine Hollands and five coarser ones, a black cap with a silver badge, a new black velvet night cap, another black cap, a hand gun (pistol), a sword and buckler, a dagger with a yellow haft and iron chain, a black frieze mantle, a canvas sack with pillow and pillow case. Quite a smart wardrobe!

It was probably at about this time that efforts were first made in the British Navy to clothe the seamen in some sort of uniform dress, but the attempts were sporadic and evidently the uniform was anything but what it purported to be. It was not until nearly two centuries later that steps were taken to introduce regulations for the dress of all grades of the navy.

The Caravel

THE CARAVEL

THE origin of the name of this type of vessel has elicited at various times considerable divergence of opinion. But the weight of modern authority is in agreement with M. Jal in ascribing the word to the Greek Κάραβος (a light vessel).

One cannot do better for a brief description of this ship than to cite this author: "The vessel so named which had a real celebrity in the XV and XVI centuries, the vessel employed by the Portuguese in their voyages of discovery and by Christopher Columbus in his daring adventure to the westward, was a small structure belonging to the family of round ships but more graceful in shape than its contemporaries, the nefs, and having narrower quarters. Also it was a faster sailer, more able, and was better fitted for all enterprises demanding speed and rapid manœuvring."

He adds that they had square sterns, fore and after castles, fairly high bulwarks, a bowsprit, and usually four masts.

The rig varied considerably according to period and nationality. The earlier caravels seem to have had no square sails although they may (after the manner of many lateen-rigged vessels) have carried a square sail on the foremast in bad weather, or for running. This practice may have established itself so firmly that later one of the several prevailing types of caravels always carried a square sail on the foremast.

This brings us to a statement of some of these variations of rig. The predominating type was a four-masted vessel with a square-rigged foremast raking well forward, having a ship's round top, and three lateen-rigged masts gradually decreasing in size. The mainmast sometimes carried a round top similar to that on the foremast, sometimes a galley form of top. Another definite type also had four masts, but the lateen and square sails were otherwise arranged. In this, the first and fourth mast carried lateen sails, while the second and third were square rigged. The exploits of the caravel were legion. Not to mention Columbus, there was the famous voyage of Bartolomé and Gonzalo Nodal in 1618 in two caravels of eighty tons each, accomplishing the circumnavigation of Tierra del Fuego; the expedition of the Emperor Charles V to Tunis in 1536, in which several caravels participated with all the pageantry and pomp to which the ships of that period so easily lent themselves; the voyage of Guillaume Le Testu (1509–72), and many others. Le Testu has left us some most interesting and reliable coloured representations of old ships, including five caravels, in his wonderful "Cosmographie Universelle."[1]

[1]See Note 4, Appendix.

The Galleon

THE GALLEON

ALMOST every untutored person who sees a model or picture of an old-time ship calls it a galleon. The reason probably is that the galleon is the type of ancient vessel most exploited in romantic literature.

The galleon was primarily a war vessel. Her "great period" was during the 16th Century and early years of the 17th Century.

Less highly charged, *i.e.*, with less decks than her companion the great or capital ship, she was more graceful of aspect and probably a better sailer. Another distinction claimed by some writers is that the decks of the galleon had three divisions or levels, while the great ship had four. One of the peculiarities of the galleon build was the form of her head. Instead of the long projecting forestage or forecastle of many of the larger ships of her time, the galleon's forecastle ended at her stem, while a long slim beak, similar to that of the galley, projected far forward. The transom of the stern was square, the poop narrow. Clench work or skids strengthened the sides, but this characteristic, while retained in Spain, Portugal, and the Spanish Netherlands seems to have passed out of fashion in English ships at an early date.

The fore and main masts were equipped with round tops

and carried courses and topsails. Galleons had also one and sometimes two lateen mizzens.

Generally speaking, the running rigging did not differ, except in degree, from that of a much later date. Reef points did not form a part of the equipment. The ship on which Sir Francis Drake died in 1596, the *Defiance,* was probably a galleon.

* * * * *

Full blow the trades adown the Spanish Main. With billowing courses, flowing topsail sheets, and mizzen well distended to the gale, with boiling foam and spouts of iridescent spray beneath her lengthy beak and forefoot broad, with gaudy pennants, and with ancient proudly flaunting in the breeze, the lordly galleon drives along the ocean's trackless plane. What heaps of tawny gold filched forth from heathen fanes her orlop holds! What glittering jewels raped from idol forms her iron-bound coffers fill! What lives have sped and tears and blood have drenched the treasure that she bears!

In vain. Afar, uplifting from the keen horizon's blade, there looms a sail. In vain. Can heron foil gerfalcon's dazzling stroke? Full soon to her eternal doom amid the waving sea-kelp's bloom shall sift the riven frames of what was once a ship; and all the remnant of her proud Castilian crew stand cowering at the terror-laden name of Drake!

An Elizabethan Ship of 1588

AN ELIZABETHAN SHIP OF 1588

PROBABLY no episode in historic times is more replete with romance than that connected with the attempt of Philip II of Spain to invade England in the year 1588 by means of his so-called Invincible Armada.

The vessels of which the Armada consisted were galleons, pataches, galleasses, zabias, galleys, and hulks, totalling, according to Hakluyt, one hundred and fifty sail including twenty caravels equipped with oars. A number of them were of considerable size. We have, in these pages, given examples of several of these types of vessels. There were sixty-four galleons of a huge "bignesse." The galleasses are stated to have been so large that they contained chambers of state, chapels, turrets, pulpits, and many features of great houses!

The English ships were not so large, but they were more seaworthy, hardier sailers, and also more numerous. The *Ark Royal,* a vessel of about eight hundred tons, was the English flagship. Another was the *Dreadnaught,* among the first of its name, in our time, a word to be applied to a class of the most formidable ships of war. The fleet opposed to the Armada consisted of one hundred and ninety-seven vessels, galleons, galleasses, galleys, pinnaces, and caravels, the smallest being but thirty tons. Only thirty-four of this number were royal vessels of war, the balance being merchant craft, fishermen, and coasters.

Lord Howard of Effingham, high admiral of the English fleet, caused the victory to be commemorated in a series of ten tapestries. These, designed by Hendrick Vroom, an eminent Dutch marine artist, and woven by Francis Speiring, were known as the Tapestry Hanging in the House of Lords. Unfortunately, they were destroyed by fire in 1834. But they had been reproduced in engravings made in 1739 by John Pine, so that we have authoritative representations of these ships as it is inconceivable that Lord Howard would have accepted Vroom's designs if they had not correctly shown the vessels composing his own fleet.

They show several of the Spanish ships propelled by oars. The vessels of the larger size thus propelled are probably meant to depict galleasses. If these were fifty-gun ships, carrying on the average one hundred and twenty-five mariners, two hundred soldiers, and three hundred galley slaves as rowers, they must have been vessels of considerable size. But the pictures show them with a freeboard, too high to be conveniently rowed, and with fore and after castles also too high for vessels of this type from what we know of their build from other and more reliable sources. Moreover, the rig is contrary to what we know to have been the rig of the Mediterranean galleasses of the period. So we feel that Vroom did not make out a very strong case in this particular. But perhaps he wished to flatter his patron, the victor in the conflict, and probably the good high admiral "fell for it," as is the saying to-day.

And what endless romances are interwoven with the aftermath of the Armada and its destruction. The Spanish ships cast away in the Orkney Islands and along the Scottish and Irish coasts in their mad dash to escape from their implacable enemies, the romances of the intermarriages between the shipwrecked Spanish mariners and the women of Scotland and Ireland.

Even to-day new romances come to light, such as the finding of a bronze breech-loading Spanish cannon fully charged, a part of the armament of the *Florencia,* a vessel of nine hundred tons, blown up in August, 1588, in Tobermary Bay, Isle of Mull, after her flight from the Channel.

The invention of Robert Louis Stevenson, in such tales as "The Merry Men," conjures up in the imagination the wild doings and far-reaching effects of this great defeat and victory.

The Cromster

THE CROMSTER

In this type, which enjoyed prominence in England during Elizabethan days and later in Holland, we find a vessel probably taking its name, according to Mr. Nance, from the shape of its stem piece.

Instead of the stem shaped like the letter "C" which may have been mentioned before as a characteristic of several Dutch vessels, the cromster's beak-head caused the stem to assume a form something like a reverse curve or flattened letter "S." The Dutch word *cromsteven*, meaning bent or crooked stem, was the name for the counterpart of this vessel as it existed in the waters of the Low Countries.

The rig seems to have consisted of three fairly constant features: a fore staysail extended upon a stay running from the masthead to the stem; a smack form of mainsail, that is, one extended upon a sprit, guyed near its middle and caused to peak up by means of a tackle rigged to its lower extremity, and a lateen mizzen.

In addition to these, a square sail on the mainmast with a small square topsail above and a spritsail were sometimes carried.

Several "square-rig" features were also embodied in the cromsters of this period. These are the six-legged martinets, formed by passing three cords through the holes of a "dead man's eye," with their accompanying hauling parts, used as brails for the mainsail (the counterparts of our bunt and leach lines of to-day), the topmast stay, set upon a sort of crow's foot passing through a piece of rope nailed to the bowsprit to receive the legs (or should we say the toes?). Another interesting feature is the peculiar yoke employed as a support to the topmast shrouds.

The cromster seems to have been particularly adaptable as a war vessel. Sir Walter Raleigh commends it as being able to carry several good-sized cannon (demiculverins).

These hoy-rigged vessels were often of considerable size, one hundred and eighty tons and more, quite as large as the *Mayflower,* their contemporary.

It is reported that such a vessel was capable of mounting sixteen or seventeen brass cannon besides iron pieces and perriers so arranged that the ordnance appeared at three different heights, and that admirals of the early 17th Century sometimes hoisted their flags aboard them in preference to square-rigged ships.

The cromster was notably too much like the hoy to permit the name to survive long as the designation of a separate class. Like so many other old-type vessels, perhaps the only place where one may now be seen (and then only in imagination) is in that mythical vortex of ancient shipping in the impenetrable centre of the grassy trap where it is claimed are gathered together in an inextricable tangle every form of ship that ever sailed the seas, from the beginning of the world down to the present day, if one will journey thither with Mr. Thomas A. Janvier in his pleasant literary vehicle entitled "The Sargasso Sea."

A Late Sixteenth Century English Ship

A LATE SIXTEENTH CENTURY
ENGLISH SHIP

No VESSEL, neither the *Santa Maria,* nor the *Constitution,* most noted and glorious of all the warships of the United States, can compare in romantic interest and patriotic reverence with the properly accorded fame of the *Mayflower.* Her name is indissolubly linked with the fundamentals of American democratic institutions. She was the wave-rocked cradle of our liberties.

And yet how little we know concerning this vessel. First of all, she was a ship, therefore had at least three masts. Her size was between 160 and 180 tons. Her master and part owner has been identified as one Christopher Jones of Rotherhithe. The name *Mayflower* was rather a common one with English vessels of her time and if the Pilgrim ship is assumed to be a *Mayflower* designated as "of London," it would seem that in 1620 she was an old vessel that had served in the anti-Armada fleet of the year 1588. The record of a *Mayflower* of London has been traced through the London port books, the Customs accounts, and the Admiralty Court records from August, 1609, to May, 1624. But there is no evidence other than the identity of the master linking this ship with the one which carried the Pilgrims to Massachusetts Bay in the latter part of the year 1620. We also know that on this trip one of the main beams amidships "bowed and cracked"; that by means of a "great iron screw" the said beam was raised again into its place and made secure by placing a post under it. We know that the *Mayflower* returned from Plymouth, Massachusetts, to England in April-May, 1621. The London port records give after this date only one entry of the ship of which Christopher Jones was master, dated October 31, 1621, when she was unloading bay salt at London from Rochelle, France. Christopher Jones died early in the year 1622 and thereafter the identity of the Pilgrim ship, in so far as the London Port records go, is lost. She was *in ruinis* at Rotherhithe in May, 1624, when, in a proceeding in the High Court of Admiralty, she was valued with her tackle and furniture at £128. This epitomizes the facts and strong probabilities relating to the history of our *Mayflower*.

As to her appearance, all must be left to conjecture. We are pretty well acquainted with the general design of hull and the particulars of the rigging of ships of the late 16th and early 17th centuries. But as to detail of structure, ornament, and interior distribution relating to the *Mayflower*, we are completely in the dark. So our illustration is fanciful to that extent.

We are indebted to Mr. R. G. Marsden for the facts based upon documentary evidence concerning the history of the *Mayflower* of London, both before and after her voyage to Plymouth. Mr. J. W. Horrocks, in a masterly article in vol. VIII (pp. 2, 81, 140, 237, and 354) of the *Mariner's Mirror* arrays the facts and draws a number of fair assumptions from them, at the same time winnowing the wheat from the chaff of bushels of suppositions, most of them ridiculous, and breaking down several theories that not all the screw-presses and posts of a fleet of *Mayflowers* as large as the Armada itself could support.

An Early Seventeenth Century Dutch Merchant Ship

AN EARLY SEVENTEENTH CENTURY
DUTCH MERCHANT SHIP

IT IS not to be wondered at that the Dutch owe much of their prosperity to the sea. Their country, once largely a part of the ocean's bed, cradled a people given practically no choice by nature in the direction of its destiny.

And the sea displays a kind and loving heart to those who woo her, even unwillingly, and leads them to fortune, albeit sometimes grudgingly and with many chastenings.

At the beginning of the 17th Century the people of the Netherlands were busy reaping the harvest of their maritime enterprise, and all were anxious to have some share in the new world. The story of Henry Hudson's voyage and ascent of the river bearing his name needs no repetition. And the name of his vessel is almost as familiar as his own.

De Halbe Moën, or *Half Moon,* was a small merchant ship differing hardly at all from the type then common in all north European countries. She exhibited the familiar lines of the late 16th Century ships: a steep sheer fore and aft, a narrow high stern transom whereon appeared the crescent moon, from which she took her name. Thereon also were the two shields displaying the lion of the United Provinces and the arms of the Dutch West Indies Company under whose ownership she sailed. The decks consisted of a short and rather steep forecastle, a waist of practically equal dimensions in length and breadth, encumbered with a ship's boat and other indispensable dunnage, a low half-deck above which appeared the rounded hood of the steerage or position of the helmsman, and above that, up the steep ascent of the half-deck (which in most of the Dutch ships followed the line of the sheer), a diminutive poop cabin.

The rigging was simple but adequate. Chains secured the lower deadeyes to the vessel's side, the chain wales being set rather low. The bowsprit was furnished with a jack staff, the immature precursor of the spritsail topmast. Rather ineffective backstays leading to the stays and crane lines were still in use. The fore and main masts bore courses with bonnets and the high narrow topsails of the period, without reef points. The continental form of jeer with the high drisse and ram's head was conspicuous, while the knave-line was still employed to circumvent the knavish tendency of the large jeer-tackle block to cable-lay. It will be recalled that a piece of cordage named a nave line in a nearly similar position was later employed to overhaul the old-fashioned trusses upon the lower yards.

Three hundred years are but a short time in the history of the civilized world, but witness what the magic of the sea has wrought in the destiny of those favoured by her! Holland has indeed lost nearly all her holdings in the western continent, but she is still far from poor and she owes practically all her wealth and prosperity directly to her maritime commerce.

The Buss

THE BUSS

As we have said elsewhere, the early sailing vessels were usually rotund. There is something compelling about this characteristic and whether it be in a person, an animal, or a vessel, liberally curved lines almost always make us react rather pleasantly, as if that quality were associated with jollity.

Well, the buss was one of those jolly-looking rotund vessels. She was replete with pleasantly full curves. The bow was rather high and the stern piece much like a segment of a circle; the poop narrow, with bulging quarters, and she had a full sweeping steer. Her rig consisted usually of three masts, the after one short and fitted with a sail employed principally for riding with her head to the wind. The fore and main masts were so equipped that they could be lowered, thus offering less resistance to the wind when the boat was riding to its nets, for these vessels were employed principally in the herring-fishing industry. Usually a single square sail was carried on each of the two larger masts, although sometimes there was a square main topsail. At times a sort of studding sail was used and occasionally a jib on a temporary bowsprit. The foresail usually had two bonnets and the mainsail one.

While the average size was from fifty to seventy tons,

busses were sometimes said to be as large as two hundred tons. The length, on the average, was fifty feet on the keel with a beam of about sixteen feet. In England during the 17th Century the maximum cost of such a vessel is said to have been about £260.

It has been said that the City of Amsterdam was built upon herrings; now, as the busses were principally employed in former times by the Dutch fishermen, in catching these same herrings and carrying them ashore, why may it not be also claimed that the buss is really the underpinning of that city? And what could be more appropriate for a Dutch *dam* than to have a floating foundation?

The Dutch Galliot

THE DUTCH GALLIOT

For some unknown reason, probably for the same one that has attributed to Homer occasional somnolent qualities, Jal has failed to include in his "Glossaire Nautique" under the head of "Galiotte," any mention of this type of vessel. Falconer likewise. But Lescallier describes it in his text and gives illustrations both of the galliot and of the koff, a vessel similar in hull but of a different rig. His text says that most of the galliots are equipped with lee boards, but his illustration of this craft does not show them.

The Dutch galliot was and still is a chubby craft having an almost perfectly circular bow and a similar stern, having also nearly flat sides. The stem piece was formed much like the letter "C." In size it varied from fifty to three hundred tons. A hundred years or more ago its rig consisted of two masts, the foremost of which with a topmast scarfed on carried a trapezoidal sail hoisted upon a gaff and a square topsail. There were several jibs extended on a quite long bowsprit having little steeve or inclination. The aftermast carried a small mizzen or dandy.

A distinction seems to have been made between the galliot and the koff, but pictures of 18th Century koffs from contemporary Dutch sources look very similar to those of galliots, as they are rigged substantially as above described.

Again, it has been authoritatively stated that koffs are both ketch rigged and schooner rigged. The illustration of the koff given in Lescallier alongside of the galliot is a sort of schooner rig supplemented by a small mast right aft with an out-rigger but with no sail thereon. This view shows lee boards. But the Dutch authority states that "the true koff has no lee boards; when she has, she is a *koff-tjalk*. Now the *tjalk* is still another sort of Dutch vessel. So we seem to be getting into deeper water than is to be found almost anywhere along the Dutch coast and so had better abandon a further discussion of the subject by concluding with a quotation of Mr. L. G. Carr-Laughton's surmise upon the matter. He says: "It seems probable therefore that the name denoted not the rig but the form of the hull or the employment of the vessel."

This latter clause interjects a new element into the already too complicated discussion. Therefore we commend any one who feels so inclined to pursue the subject further in the language of the land of origin of these vessels, and if he is successful in mastering the intricacies of its naval terminology and in extricating us from the hole into which we have fallen, he is certainly entitled to high praise as being able to "beat the Dutch."

An English Capital Ship of The Early Seventeenth Century

AN ENGLISH CAPITAL SHIP OF THE EARLY SEVENTEENTH CENTURY

TRAGEDY may be called one of the children of romance. And the *Sovereign of the Seas* is part and parcel of one of the grimmest tragedies ever enacted in the annals of any country.

When Charles I ascended the English throne in the year 1625, he seemed indeed the favourite of fortune. Endowed with a fine mind, accomplished, a gentleman to the tips of his fingers, assuming the reins of government at a time when the great strides made in the commerce of his kingdom and the budding colonies in the New World required governmental encouragement to the shipping of the realm, it was obvious that, to a man of his intellectual capacity, the navy should have been an object of especial solicitude.

Scientific principles were being applied to ship-building in England as well as elsewhere in Europe. The Pett family, hereditary naval architects, as it were, to the royal family since the days of Henry VII, was at this time represented by Phineas Pett, father, and Peter, his son. The laws of the motion of solid bodies through fluids were studied and applied. Experiments and rule of thumb were giving place to scientific methods.

The *Royal Prince,* one of the finest and largest vessels

launched up to that time, apparently only served to urge Charles to improve upon improvement. He duly commissioned his shipwrights, including Phineas Pett, to build a larger and still finer vessel.

The result was the planning of the *Sovereign of the Seas.* Launched in 1637 this vessel was one of the largest seagoing ships theretofore ever constructed. Nor was her size more remarkable than were her ornamentations. Covered from stem to stern with most elaborate wood-carvings, her long bead-head crowned with a mounted effigy of King Edgar, the conqueror of Saxon England, trampling under his charger's hoofs seven fallen monarchs whose shorn beards bordered his mantle, the many badges of honour ennobling its sides, a cupid riding a lion terminating the stem-head, the curved forecastle (Pett's latest invention) displaying an elaborate allegory of the ideals of his Royal Master, the astronomical panels along the vessel's sides, the glories of Olympus with its gods and goddesses displayed on the quarter galleries, the still more splendid stern, embellished with other allegorical and biblical figures, designed to represent the ship's glorious career, the whole blazing with gold and colour, the possible but not too probable royals, the endless streamers, picturesque but hardly practical, all combined to form an effect of pomp and promise as radiant as the King's own.

But alas, the very measures which made for greatness and romance made also for ruin. Everyone knows the story of the resistance to the collection of the ship money tax, of Charles's insistence upon his divine right to override constitutional government, of the rebellion, the revolution, and of the sad procession to the block at Whitehall on January 30, 1649.

The *Sovereign of the Seas* was no more a success in her element than her royal originator was upon the land. During the Commonwealth she was mutilated by losing, like the monarch, not her head, but by being cut down a whole deck, because she had proved to be top-heavy.

Laid up for a complete rebuilding at Chatham in 1696, she was totally destroyed by fire.

An English Sixty-Gun Ship of About The Year 1670

AN ENGLISH SIXTY-GUN SHIP OF ABOUT THE YEAR 1670

THE war vessels of two hundred and fifty years ago were rated according to the number of guns carried.

Generally speaking, at about this time, a vessel of one hundred guns and upward was called in some navies a ship of the first rate; those having in the neighbourhood of ninety guns, second rates; those having from sixty to eighty guns, third rates; from fifty to sixty guns, fourth rates, and so on. Ships having fifty guns or more were designated as ships of the line, i. e., those which fought in the line of battle, as vessels of less than fifty guns were not generally supposed to be placed in that position.

Ships of the line usually carried their batteries on two or more decks. The figures as to armament given above were flexible and varied both as to locality and period.

Prominent among the various appliances with which all vessels were from most remote times equipped, was that required for raising the anchor. Several machines were in use, but the most generally employed was the capstan. Nearly everyone is familiar with that piece of machinery. It consists of an upright cylinder rotated on an axis in the vertical plane of the vessel's keel by means of levers called capstan bars. The anchor cable or other rope to which power is to be applied passes three or more times around the capstan, and as the hands walk around pushing on the capstan bars, other hands, continually holding the rope taut, gather in the slack. The capstan bars were formerly held in place by a light rope passing through horizontal holes in their extremities. This rope was called a swifter.

To show an example of the complexity of marine terminology, there were not less than three sorts of swifters used on a ship.

The Leconsfield Manuscript, an early 17th Century treatise upon the rigging of ships, thus describes another variety of swifter: "Thei ar as big as the shrowdes and fastened to the head of the mast and chaine wales as the shrowdes. Ther ar 2, on[e] on each side. They serue only to stay the mast and beare with the shrowdes." This means that they constitute the first or the furthest forward of any set of lower shrouds.

In order to tighten the shrouds quickly when it was not feasible to set up on the lanyards in the deadeyes, another device was employed. A single block was seized inboard at the same height (about twenty feet above the deck) to each shroud. A rope also called a swifter was then passed back and forth diagonally between these blocks so that each in turn was brought into the system. When the swifter was boused taut, it constricted all the shrouds equally on both sides by hauling both sets inboard, thus taking in any slackness. This custom was pretty generally followed until wire rigging superseded the old fibre cordage.

The Flute

THE FLUTE

DURING the 17th Century the flute was the high chieftain-ess of the round-sterned tribe. As a carrier, she seems to have replaced the hulk among the traders of northern and western countries.

In appearance, her peculiarities were marked. In the early years of the 17th Century one would have seen a stubby stiff bow extending into a form of curved beak, just then very much the style. A side view would have shown a well-curved sheer with a stern which rounded generously to the stem post as high as the top of the rudder. Above this an abnormally narrow and lofty transom was joined by steep rising sides to form a much constricted poop.

Between these upper and lower parts of the stern and di-viding them transversely one would find that peculiar hol-low or cove which shows as a characteristic of so many of the ships of the 14th and 15th centuries.

The flute was ship rigged, and as such her development in rig was upon similar terms with her square-tucked and round-tucked sisters. There were no marked peculiarities in this respect to differentiate it from other ships of the period. Many of the later flutes were armed, and it may be that it is perhaps because their guns were carried upon a single deck that there arose the expression, armed *en flûte,* referring to a ship with guns upon its upper deck only, the lower decks being used for the stowage of goods, horses, troops, etc.; in other words, an armed transport. There seems, however, no particular reason why the flute should have been selected to furnish this term to fit such a combination. Any other ship-rigged vessel carrying guns upon a single deck would have served as well. It is a problem that will have to be left to the etymologists.

The flute seems to have been a popular form of hull, as many contemporary representations of her appear in the prints and paintings of nearly all the countries of western Europe. Mr. Nance tells us that it was in such ships as this that the tar, timber, and other articles which Holland could not produce for her own ships would be brought from the north in exchange for manufactures and goods imported in her bottoms from far-distant regions. It was a favourite form in Holland, a land of round-sterned vessels, and it is more than probable that many flutes crossed to America and performed important rôles in the development of the Dutch colonies in the new world. So far as is known to the author, no particular vessel of those whose names are recorded has been identified as a flute. Perhaps records still exist that would furnish this information if occasion demanded.

A Late Seventeenth Century French Ship of the First Rate

A LATE SEVENTEENTH CENTURY FRENCH SHIP OF THE FIRST RATE

WHILE a considerable advance in size has been made during the latter part of the 17th Century in the French ships, owing to the intelligence and energy of Colbert and Louvois, the able ministers of Louis XIV, in England and in Holland the tonnage of the larger vessels of war was not materially greater than at the beginning of the century.

The *Sovereign of the Seas,* until her destruction in 1696, one of the largest vessels of the British Navy, measured about one thousand six hundred tons. The *Duke,* launched in 1685, measured one thousand five hundred and forty-six tons; the *Royal William,* launched in 1692, had a tonnage of one thousand three hundred and forty. These were all first-rate ships. The last named ship was never a success. She was cranky and carried her guns badly. Sir Cloudsley Shovel, one of the most brilliant officials of the time, complained bitterly of the poor construction and equipment of the English vessels.

Not so the larger French ships of this period. The *Soleil Royal,* one hundred and eight guns, was of one thousand nine hundred and forty tons; the *Royal Louis* measured about one thousand eight hundred tons.

Moreover, the French ships had better lines, were

roomier, and carried their guns to more advantage. Artistically also at this time they were far superior to their contemporaries.

Such great sculptors as Nicolas Lavray and Pierre Puget laboured to extend the glory and magnificence of Le Grand Monarque by lavishing the richness of their imagination upon the embellishment of the ships of Le Roi Soleil, while a no less famous person than the King's own painter, Le Brun, designed the ornament for the *Soleil Royal*.

Many of Puget's original designs for ship decorations are preserved in the Musée du Louvre as well as several superb pieces of wood carving executed (for a like purpose) by his own hand.

His designs for the great ship's lanterns carried at the stern are particularly graceful. We show in the appendix several forms as employed in different countries at about this period. These beacons gleaming across the waves at night lighted up the richly gilded ornament on the sterns of the great fabrics as they moved majestically beneath the silent stars or under cloud-swept, tempestuous skies, the harbingers of romance and the playthings of royal ambition.

A Dutch Ship of the End of the Seventeenth Century

A DUTCH SHIP OF THE END OF THE
SEVENTEENTH CENTURY

IT MAY be of interest to make a few comparisons between
the ships of the United Provinces with the contemporaneous
vessels of other European countries during that most interesting period in the development of naval architecture,
the last decades of the 17th Century.

The ships of Holland during this epoch were on the whole
somewhat smaller than those of the more formidable of her
naval rivals—France, Spain, and England—based upon an
approximately equal rating so far as armament is concerned.
Again, they had much flatter floors with more square bilges
and drew less water in order to clear the shoals abounding
near the coast of the Low Countries. Their forefoot had
considerably more rake. The beak-head was usually longer.
The sterns varied in construction, although the Dutch methods seem to have been patterned to a certain extent upon the
French. The dissimilarity of treatment of the ornament
upon the sterns made them look quite unlike. The forecastle
bulkhead in the Dutch ships showed a marked variance
from the English both in form and in relation to the cat-
heads. Another peculiarity of the Dutch ships is the "clap-
board" effect of their clinker-built upper works.

In the rigging, some difference may be also noted. The

masthead caps of the Dutch ships were much wider, and in side view showed a sort of serpentine line, being considerably thicker in the aftermost portion. This thickened curved part was so designed in order to carry without too much nipping the jeers passing over it instead of through large blocks which in the English ships hung below the cap. The form of the combined lift and sheet block at the end of the yards was also notably different.

Sometimes it is difficult to differentiate between some of the Dutch and Scandinavian vessels because the Danish and Swedish shipwrights followed Dutch methods closely, while Peter the Great of Russia actually worked in the shipyards of the Netherlands in order to be able to reproduce their methods in his own country.

The Ketch

THE KETCH

LIKE many variations from more or less fixed and permanent species, the evolution of the ketch also shows us marked changes from time to time in a type which was itself a derivation (so far as rig goes) from the three-masted ship.

Probably no more apt concept of a ketch can be formulated than that employed by Mr. R. Morton Nance, "a ship without a foremast." To trace the etymology of the term "ketch" would be perhaps almost as complex as to define and state in order its many successive changes in rig and hull. It may be stated with reasonable assurance that the word is derived from the 15th Century English word "cache" as applied to a cargo boat, being the same in its older form as a "catch."

Glanville (1625) tells us that "catches being short and round built, be verie apt" (convenient, not liable) "to turn up and downe, and useful to goe to and fro and to carry messages between shipp and shipp, almost with any wind."

We know little of the early rig of ketches and perhaps, as is so often the case in early times, the word applied originally to the form of hull rather than to the rig.

At all events, it is not until we arrive at the 17th Century that we are upon at all firm ground. This would seem rather of an Irishism in treating a subject so closely identified with such an unstable element as the sea. That which holds our interest more than anything else in connection with ketches is a twofold development of the rig, for we may disregard differences of hull and, in so far as the limits of this article goes, confine ourselves to a discussion of the vessel's apparel.

The ketch rig in a way became at an early date closely associated with what would then have been called a yacht hull. But the vessel would then have been called a yacht only if it were hoy rigged; if, on the other hand, the vessel had square yards and a mizzen, it was called a ketch.

As an illustration of the variation in terminology and as demonstrating how the requirements of a particular usage may effect a certain type of craft, the necessity of providing a space free from obstructions, for use as a floating mortar battery, may be considered. A vessel without a foremast, with a mainmast stepped amidship, with a mizzenmast, both masts rigged similarly to a ship, and with a stout chain for a mainstay, the forward part of the vessel being equipped with mortars having a free range abeam and forward, was called a *galliote à bombes* in France and a bomb ketch in England. Both the French and the English types were usually pink sterned. The French example naturally enough took its name from the Dutch galliot.

The illustration shows the rig at its nearest point of contact with the late 17th Century and early 18th Century vessels.[1]

[1]See Note 5, Appendix.

An Eighteenth Century Seventy-Four Gun Ship

AN EIGHTEENTH CENTURY SEVENTY-FOUR GUN SHIP

THE ship of seventy-four guns may be said to have been, during the "great period" of wooden sailing ships, the man-of-war par excellence. It was the most popular sized ship among the great European naval powers as is evidenced by the fact that at the end of the 18th Century there were more seventy-fours both in the English and in the French Navy than ships of any other class. The word class is here intended to mean any particular type of approximately a like tonnage having the same number of guns. Thus the frigates, while collectively more numerous, varied considerably in size and in the number of guns carried.

Mr. John Masefield has said that a modern sailor, accustomed to the keen iron ships of the present day, would have called such a ship a "sea-wagon," qualified or otherwise, before spitting and passing by. But when the great sails were set, and the hull began to move through the water, the cumbrous fabric took on attributes of beauty and nobility. There has been perhaps no such beautiful thing on earth, the work of man's hands, as an old seventy-four under sail.

Antiquity may lend charm and romance to the edifices erected on land by the great architects and artisans of the past, but how much more charm and romance surrounds those masterpieces of the naval architects and constructors of bygone days, those creations, destined to struggle against the destructive forces of winds and waves, of fire, or treacherous shoals and uncharted rocks, those structures whose very lack of permanence in substance has been the means of strengthening the memory of their beauty in the mind of man!

The French seventy-fours were not substantially different from their peers (or should we say peeresses?) in other navies. There was, however, one feature quite distinctive, the form of the stern transom. At this period, the outline of their sterns above the lowest member was almost a perfect ellipse. Otherwise, at a distance it would have taken a practised eye to discern such differences of rig as existed. These fine distinctions are as intangible and yet as manifest to the trained eye as are the differences to be noted in old porcelain and glass by that of the connoisseur. If you had asked an old sailor how he recognized such and such a vessel as being of this or that nationality, he would probably have answered "by the cut of her jib." This subtle differentiation would have left most folks not much wiser than before.

Most of the larger French ships of the end of the 18th Century had built-in waists; that is, wide permanent structures joining the forecastle and the quarter deck. In the English ships there were sometimes light removable gangways serving as a means of communication on the same plane between these two parts of the vessel, but in many others a person passing between these stations would have been compelled to descend one ladder and to ascend another. The illustration shows a French seventy-four, the *Terrible*, captured by the British about the year 1747.

An East Indiaman of 1750

AN EAST INDIAMAN OF 1750

"The Governor and Company of Merchants of London trading to the East Indies," as was the early official name of the Honourable East India Company. It was a creature of high privilege. Chartered in the year 1600, it maintained its lucrative and exclusive trade, sternly suppressing all competition by other British subjects—"interlopers" they were called—until its unrepublican character at last penetrated the callousness of English statesmen at the end of the 18th Century.

The Company's ships were well armed and heavily manned. Pirates both of eastern and western provenance were always to be feared, while the numerous wars in which England participated during the term of the Company's existence rendered it necessary to be well prepared for emergency.

It was in the form and build of the hull that the Indiamen differed from the contemporary warships. As cargo carriers, the full underbodies, flat floors, sharp turns of the bilges and quick rises, stamped them as slower and more capacious fabrics.

Again there were many practices in rigging peculiar to the merchant service. To cite some instances, one might mention the form of halyards, of some of the stays, the fittings of studding-sail booms, and the lead of many ropes.

Studding-sails were one of the stand-bys of the Eastern trader. With fair winds and good weather, they sometimes sailed incredible distances without changing the position of a tack or sheet, although sail was always shortened at night.

The illustration shows a ship which might be easily taken at first glance for a war vessel. But if we could have a look at the arrangement of the decks, we would soon see a decided difference.

Fortunes were quickly acquired in this commerce, in which the ship's master not infrequently shared, for he was, under certain conditions, permitted to trade on his own account in a space in the ship's hold especially set aside for him. A single voyage often netted the master as much as £10,000!

Richly dowered daughters were common among the East India merchant princes, whose dollars matched and overmatched patents of nobility and decorations. If the romance of many of the marriages of money with position waned with the honeymoon, there was enough of it in the wealth of the Indies to lure new generations to the same practices.

And the long voyages to and from far-off Bombay and Calcutta, with the blue boundless ocean stretching out on all sides, the constant companionship, the occasional days and nights of terror, all were rare settings to affect young and impressionable hearts. And if this sort of romance is not the true romance of the sea, it is at all events its certain corollary and the foundation of many a happening which no one would hesitate to call romantic.

The Lugger

THE LUGGER

Next to the galleon there is probably no old-time vessel which appears to appeal more strongly to the popular imagination than does the lugger.

Nearly everyone is familiar with the quotation from the time-honoured melodrama uttered in a stage whisper, "Once aboard the pirate lugger and the girl is ours!" For the lugger has been long associated in fancy and in fact as well with piracy, smuggling, and deeds of violence.

With their lugsails flattened like boards, these craft not only out-pointed but out-sailed the lumbering revenue cutters set to the task of catching them, with as little chance as the proverbial snowball in the infernal regions. So much so that by an English statute the beam of luggers was so regulated that it was a crime to build or operate one of too narrow dimensions. And as a necessary corollary, armed luggers were introduced into the custom's service on the principle of setting a thief to catch a thief.

A chart published as early as 1586 shows a two-masted vessel with what appears to be a lugsail forward equipped with vangs and a bonnet, a bowsprit, a spritsail, and a lateen mizzen sheeted to an outrigger.

Lugsails are also mentioned by many of the writers of the 16th and 17th centuries.

An early picture of a lugger (1794) shows a three-masted craft with lug topsails on the fore and main carried upon topmasts erected behind their respective masts.

There are two theories advanced for the origin of the lugsail, some claiming that it is a lateen sail bereft of its forward apex, while others contend that it was derived from the square sail, the yard of which, at its point of juncture with the mast, being fastened at a point approximately one third of its distance from one end instead of at the middle. As the sail was in vogue in both southern and northern waters, both claims may be correct.

The luggers before the days of steam navigation were the furnishers of the fleets anchored in bad weather in the Downs and other harbours of the Channel ports. They were also great wreckers and slavers. It is believable that from their extortionate charges for these services they easily earned an unenviable reputation as pirates to which their associated trade in contraband contributed not a little.

The Hówker

THE HOWKER

Of the round-sterned genus and a near relation of the buss and the dogger, was the howker. This spelling is preferred to hooker, because Mr. H. S. Vaughan has pointed out, with considerable force, that the English and Irish fishing boats really receive this name because they are generally employed in fishing with hooks and lines.

So that we will confine ourselves to discussing the 17th and 18th Century craft of the name, the *Houcre* or *Hourque* of the French and the *Hoecker* of the Dutch, when the howker was a ship of burden ranging in size from fifty to two hundred tons.

The earliest illustration of what may be a howker is to be found in the original *Mariner's Mirror* of 1588. In the year 1669 there were armed French vessels of this description. Van Yk (1699) gives the design of a *hoecker* for the East India service, and the three 18th Century writers, Aubin (1702), Lescallier (1777), and Steele (1794), all give cuts of the type. The hull had a rounded stubby bow, a curved stern, a high rudder with a tiller coming in above the stern post, double wales, and often a cabin aft under a small poop deck.

The rig varied somewhat according to period and locality, but by the beginning of the 18th Century resembled closely the ketch of the period. Lescallier's and Steele's illustrations show a pole mainmast but the mizzen topmast is a separate spar. The bowsprit was rigged to one side of the stem and could probably be hauled inboard.

After the year 1800 the term howker seems to have been applied to many one-masted vessels, probably for the reason, as pointed out by Messrs Alan Moore and R. Morton Nance in their admirable article upon this vessel in the November, 1911, issue of the *Mariner's Mirror,* p. 293, that the trading howker had become obsolete. They state that in its other form the word "hooker," which they employ, has a colloquial meaning as "packet." This does not agree with our New England nautical slang. "Hooker," with the seafaring folk of the eastern coast of the United States, is a term of contempt. Many years ago, when, as a boy, the writer expressed his admiration for a certain schooner hailing from Tuckertown in Barnegat Boy, his mentor, Captain Adelbert Cramer, from whom were acquired his first instruction and interest in affairs nautical, spat vigorously to leeward, and remarked contemptuously, "That old hooker!" leaving his pupil abashed.

The Bugalet

THE HOWKER

OF THE round-sterned genus and a near relation of the buss and the dogger, was the howker. This spelling is preferred to hooker, because Mr. H. S. Vaughan has pointed out, with considerable force, that the English and Irish fishing boats really receive this name because they are generally employed in fishing with hooks and lines.

So that we will confine ourselves to discussing the 17th and 18th Century craft of the name, the *Houcre* or *Hourque* of the French and the *Hoecker* of the Dutch, when the howker was a ship of burden ranging in size from fifty to two hundred tons.

The earliest illustration of what may be a howker is to be found in the original *Mariner's Mirror* of 1588. In the year 1669 there were armed French vessels of this description. Van Yk (1699) gives the design of a *hoecker* for the East India service, and the three 18th Century writers, Aubin (1702), Lescallier (1777), and Steele (1794), all give cuts of the type. The hull had a rounded stubby bow, a curved stern, a high rudder with a tiller coming in above the stern post, double wales, and often a cabin aft under a small poop deck.

The rig varied somewhat according to period and locality, but by the beginning of the 18th Century resembled closely the ketch of the period. Lescallier's and Steele's illustrations show a pole mainmast but the mizzen topmast is a separate spar. The bowsprit was rigged to one side of the stem and could probably be hauled inboard.

After the year 1800 the term howker seems to have been applied to many one-masted vessels, probably for the reason, as pointed out by Messrs Alan Moore and R. Morton Nance in their admirable article upon this vessel in the November, 1911, issue of the *Mariner's Mirror,* p. 293, that the trading howker had become obsolete. They state that in its other form the word "hooker," which they employ, has a colloquial meaning as "packet." This does not agree with our New England nautical slang. "Hooker," with the seafaring folk of the eastern coast of the United States, is a term of contempt. Many years ago, when, as a boy, the writer expressed his admiration for a certain schooner hailing from Tuckertown in Barnegat Boy, his mentor, Captain Adelbert Cramer, from whom were acquired his first instruction and interest in affairs nautical, spat vigorously to leeward, and remarked contemptuously, "That old hooker!" leaving his pupil abashed.

The Bugalet

THE BUGALET

Another small square-rigged craft formerly in use along the coasts of Brittany was the bugalet. The name was known in the 17th Century. The rig formerly consisted of two masts, the after one much larger than the other, bearing a large square sail surmounted by a topsail. The foremast, much smaller than the other, also carried a square sail much smaller in area than the after lower sail. There was no top-sail on this mast. The boat was also equipped with a bow-sprit set with one or two jibs.

In later times its rig was much similar to the English brigs. The date of its appearance seems to be unknown, as well as the derivation of the name.

In the manuscript archives giving the "Condition of the French Marine" for the year 1690 and included among the "Bastiments Interiompus," i. e., those not included in the regular classification of vessels, two bugalets, or *models de vaisseau,* are reported as being at Brest. Why they should have been referred to as models of ships of the line, as the word *vaisseau* was then commonly employed, is difficult to understand because this small boat has little in common with the capital ship of the period.

The greater convenience of the fore and aft rig, especially for smaller vessels, together with its greater efficiency when sailing close to the wind, probably accounts for the disappearance of many of the smaller square-rigged craft.

The profession of the sailor is one of the most conservative in the world, particularly among such an immobile race as the Bretons, and it would not be safe to assert that some examples of the bugalet do not still exist along the Brittany littoral. No record, however, of even a recent use of the word has rewarded the researches of the author.

An Eighteenth Century Frigate

AN EIGHTEENTH CENTURY FRIGATE

W HILE the word "frigate" is in itself not in anywise associated with the notion of decks, it is that portion of the ship's structure which immediately becomes important in any discussion of the type of vessel bearing that name.

It seems improbable that the decks of the very early ships were flush, that is, that they ran from end to end of the ship without a rise or fall somewhere. If we consider the evidence furnished by the concrete examples of ancient Scandinavian ships actually before us, we see that they had short decks forward and aft at about the same level relative to the keel and a long lower one amidships. The question of the level of decks has aroused a great deal of controversy. Without expressing an opinion upon the correctness of the several contentions, it is unquestionably a fact that at a comparatively early day a new style of arrangement of decks made its appearance. This was accomplished by the installation of a continuous platform running from end to end of the ship without a break. Such a manner of construction was called "frigate fashion." Once introduced, the idea took hold rapidly. The earlier ships constructed by Peter Pett in the beginning of the 17th Century were said to be built in this wise, notably the *Sovereign of the Seas* of 1637.

On May 3, 1696, Sir Peter Pett wrote a letter to Mr.

Samuel Pepys in which he said, "Many years ago I gave Sir Christopher Wren the draught of an old-fashioned ship and another of the frigate fashion that he might see the difference of them."

The term "frigate" in its more restricted sense is quite another matter. Normally, and disregarding earlier applications of the term, the word has been used to describe one of the smaller types of warships, one having, say, from twenty-four to fifty cannon. This armament was carried on flush decks. Some of the smaller frigates were provided with oars as a supplementary means of propulsion.

The frigate was more or less of an ocean free lance. Many of them were designed for speed and they were particularly efficient as commerce destroyers. During the latter years of the 18th Century the French led the world in designing ships, and their models were willingly followed by both English and American naval constructors.

Josiah Humphreys, in designing the first three American frigates, *Constitution, Constellation,* and *United States,* launched in 1797, followed what he called "the best French method."

The numerous single-handed combats between frigate and frigate are among the most stirring narrations in the annals of naval warfare. When steam power was introduced into naval vessels, many of the frigates were equipped with steam. With the coming of armour plate, the type disappeared, and now, with the exception of a few examples preserved for their historical interest, they have ceased to exist.

The Felucca

THE FELUCCA

THE Mediterranean Sea has been one of the great mothers of ships. Her children have been quite as numerous as the proverbial old woman who lived in a shoe. But unlike that prolific but futile female, she has known exactly what to do with her children during all the ages.

From the earliest times to the present the landlocked, tideless sea has developed and multiplied her progeny, sending them to the uttermost ends of the earth, enriching them, chastening them, fostering them. There have been quarrels among them, as is ever the fashion in large families, many have died off, and of some lines many have changed so that even their sisters would not know them now.

Among the strongest of the stock was the galley with its great lateen sails, and to this family belongs the felucca. Jal derives the name from the generic Turkish word "fulk," meaning a ship, and this seems a likely source.

Of the vessel itself, many have been the varieties classed under the name, sometimes with one mast and a triangular sail, at others bearing two masts with lateen sails, some with oars and some without them.

The characteristic Catalanean *felouque* of Jal's day with masts inclined well forward, equipped with high triangular sails, often had, on each side of the stem, a painted eye after the style of those which ornamented the prows of the ancient Egyptian and Greek ships. The lateen sail with its high pointing whippy yard is much better suited to the lighter and dryer winds of the south than to the heavier airs of the northern seas. At the slightest increase of velocity the yard bends, spilling the wind, to resume its lofty position when the gust passes, and ready again to catch the faintest zephyr.

It is a poetic word, felucca, and worthy to have been celebrated in verses such as were written by the immortal bard of progress, Byron. And an association never to be forgotten is that the felucca was the craft that bore to his death Byron's ill-fated friend, the gentle Shelley.

With its sails set upon opposite sides when running free before the wind, like hare's ears, as the French say, it lends its unfailing picturesqueness to every glimpse of the sea, a snowy spot upon the aquamarine waters, recalling to such of us as are willing to listen the many romances of the Mediterranean, the cradle of our western civilization.

The Barque Provençale

THE BARQUE PROVENÇALE

Small craft in great variety are to be found everywhere in the Mediterranean differing both in the form of hull and in apparel. Many of these are quite generally called barks, but the term is generic.

In southern Europe the inclination toward the lateen sail was strong and as we have noted elsewhere, with good reason. But the lateen may there be seen combined with both square and fore and aft sails.

The *barque provençale* did not differ materially from other small vessels, called elsewhere than along the shores of the Mediterranean by other names.

Characteristics of the galley were incorporated into the hull of the barque, notably in the beak, useful in providing a stout support for the rigging employed in operating the forward portion of the long antennæ of the lateen sail nearest the bow. The mainmasts of these barks usually consisted of a straight pole, *à pible,* with three yards rigged after the manner of the poleacre. The foremast, as may be seen, is the lateen dear to the hearts of the mariners of the Mediterranean Sea, the heritage of centuries. It is a cumbersome sail to handle, but that seems to make no difference to the conservative mind of the sailor man. Often smaller lateen sails on shorter yards were substituted in place of the larger ones as occasion demanded, this being a simple way of shortening sail, although it would seem as if the larger lateen, with its long yard, when removed to make way for its smaller substitute, would be more or less "in the way" when lying on deck.

The skippers of these small craft were and are hardy and bold but usually ignorant of even the fundamentals of navigation. Quite often they cruise without even a compass, but on such voyages it is safe to say that they never venture out of sight of land.

The writer recalls seeing a few years ago, drawn out on the beach at Amalfi in Italy, a number of boats designated by the natives as *barche* (barks) ranging between ten and sixty tons. In nearly all of the hulls archaic forms could be seen. They were decorated in most florid fashion. Many had "eyes" painted on their sides near the stem. The diversity of rig was noticeable. Fore and aft sails were in the majority, but the lateen rig was still retained by a few. Unfortunately, there was nothing in the gathering that in any wise resembled the square-rigged barques of a century ago.[1]

[1]See Note 6, Appendix.

The Tartane

THE TARTANE

BAUGEAN says that the name of tartane is applied quite generally in the Mediterranean to medium-sized vessels having one large mast and a small mizzen, the latter either carrying a square sail or a lateen. His illustrations of tartanes do not bear him out, however, and what he probably meant to say was that the mainmast sometimes carried a square sail or a lateen or perhaps both. In his view of the Neapolitan tartane, he shows us a vessel similar to our illustration, while in another picture we see a small two-masted vessel with a large lateen on the mainmast, above which appears a square topsail and above that a top gallant of two triangular parts, one on each side of the mast. This latter is a Mediterranean form, dating back to Roman times. (Compare the Roman *corbita,* page 50.)

It will be seen that it is the small mizzen of the Neapolitan craft which carries the lateen, while the mainmast is fitted with square sails on a pole mast or *à pible.* It may be noted also that the jib is a very large one, carried upon a sprit extending a short distance beyond the pronounced elongation of the stem—a decided galley feature.

Another reminder of the galley is the structure consisting of two boards, one on each side, projecting aft from the stern, joining some distance from the hull, and serving as the support for the outrigger pole, to the extremity of which is affixed the block for the sheet of the mizzen. This extension, sometimes very elaborately ornamented, is to be seen also in the craft of many Mediterranean countries, including those of Turkey. The mizzenmast also serves to hold the brace blocks of the two upper square yards of the mainmast.

The hull of this tartane is drawn in at the stern rather sharply so that the craft is really a double-ender. Notice that the stern post comes all the way up to the top of the after-deck. The rudder head rises above this end and the tiller leads forward between the sides of the outrigger structure, also a very ancient form.

Many of the lateen-rigged craft, when the wind became too heavy for these large triangular sails to be carried safely, lowered them and hoisted a short square sail in their place. The small tartane described above was so equipped that such a substitution could be quickly effected. The combinations of the lateen with other forms of sail would appear to be infinite and yet the ingenuity of the Mediterranean sailor seems to have made use of nearly all of them.

The Norwegian Cat

THE NORWEGIAN CAT

THE word "cat" has for many centuries had a wide application in marine terminology. First of all, it was applied in the 13th Century to a species of rowing vessel having a beak like a galley, two lateral steering oars, and propelled by a hundred sweeps, each rowed by two men.

Again (and this is the subject of our illustration), a cat was the name of a merchant vessel of northern Europe, something like the Dutch flute, having very full rounded quarters and blunt bows, with little rake to the stem and stern pieces and with flat floors. Such a vessel was only a sort of tub designed to hold as much cargo as possible. Naturally, it sailed slowly and was sluggish in a seaway.

The rigging was simple. Three pole masts without tops supported lower and topsail yards so arranged in Aubin's time (1702) that the yard and sails could be lowered to the deck in lieu of furling them aloft. This method made for economy of operation, as these simple evolutions could be performed by a small crew. Lescallier mentions that sometimes top gallants were set flying above the topsails.

Another boat to which was given the name cat, or *chatte* (the feminine form of the word in French), was a sort of lighter employed in loading and discharging larger vessels.

We might mention also our own catboat as a distinctive type.

Cat is a favourite word with seamen. The cat-head taking its name probably from the ornament usually sculptured on the extremity of the stout projecting beam designed to keep the anchor when a-weigh well out from the ship's hull, naturally and obviously led to the use of the term to "cat" the anchor.

The instrument of punishment called the cat is too well known to need description. The cat-hole was another name for the top or lubber's hole.

Cat harpings were the ropes used to constrict the shrouds at the hounds so that the yards could be more sharply braced.

Among this large family of cats one would think that a mouse would be in great danger of meeting a sudden and tragic end. And yet an extended and somewhat careful perusal of naval literature and technical marine treatises has failed to disclose that any such catastrophe (if the pun may be permitted) ever happened from such a cause to any mouse on the old hemp-rigged vessels—for they all harboured several of these rodents as a regular and necessary part of their equipment. For the benefit of the uninitiated it may be stated that a mouse was an enlargement worked with rope yarns designed to retain in place the eye of the stay, thereby forming a loop or collar about the masthead.

The Bilander

THE BILANDER

THE name of this vessel, also spelled be'landre and by-lander, seems to have appeared in England as far back as the reign of Queen Elizabeth.

Like so many other words used to designate a type of vessel, it has been applied in many different localities to quite dissimilar craft and may refer to either the form of hull, the rig, or the use to which the vessel is put. Several of the 18th Century marine writers agree in representing it as here shown. Its distinguishing feature was its large trapezoidal mainsail somewhat resembling an early ship's lateen mizzen, the forward end of which came as far forward as the middle of the ship.

Lescallier (1777) mentions that this sail was hoisted by a "drisse," and while he does not say that this "drisse" or halyard was operated by means of a "sep" or knight-head, it may, nevertheless, prove interesting to discuss this ancient item of rigging.

In early times the lower yards of ships were not stationary as they are to-day, but were raised or lowered as occasion demanded. Rectangular cloths called bonnet and drabler were laced successively to the lower side of the course and enlarged this sail, or when removed shortened it, for it must be remembered that for several centuries reef points gathering up the head of the sail to the yard were not employed.

Lowering the yard also lowered the centre of effort of the reduced canvas and so eased the vessel in a high wind. For the purpose of changing the position of the yards, powerful machinery was needed. A stout rectangular post, securely fastened at as low a point as possible, projected a distance of four or five feet above the main deck abaft the mast. This was pierced longitudinally usually with four slots containing sheeves all rotating on the same axis. This constituted the lower portion of the tackle.

The upper portion consisted of a very large block, sometimes called a ram's head, having four sheeves below and another sheeve at right angles thereto above. The yard tye, also called the jeer, was reeved as follows: One end was fastened to the yard at the slings; it then passed through a block depending from the masthead or through a large sheeve on one side of the hounds, then through the upper cross-sheeve in the ram's head, up through the block at the masthead and down again to the yard where the end was hitched at the slings. The tackle was then united by the haulyard passing successively through the said four lower sheeves of the ram's head and three of the sheeves in the "sep" or knight head. The fourth sheeve in the knight head was customarily employed as a lead for the top rope. The knight head mentioned took its name from the custom of embellishing the upper portion of the "sep" with such a decoration, as was the practice also with bowsprit bollards. These still retain their romantic name, although their position and functions have changed.[1]

[1] See Note 7, Appendix.

147

The Fire Ship

THE FIRE SHIP

FROM the most remote times fire was resorted to in naval conflicts as a natural weapon. Bundles of blazing materials were hurled from positions of vantage, while at an early date powerful combustibles such as the famous Greek fire were employed.

Later it became the custom to make use of specially designed and equipped ships for this purpose. The plan was to isolate the forward part of the vessel from a point slightly abaft the mainmast where a very thick bulkhead of heavy wooden beams was built across from side to side. Other thick partitions with very heavy tight-fitting doors surrounded the waist while the upper deck was also stoutly protected against the rapid spread of the flames upward.

Near the fire ports opening out of this enclosed portion of the lower deck troughs were built with wooden tubes running to the ports. These troughs were filled with highly inflammable liquids, and bombs were sometimes placed near the openings, so that, upon exploding, the fire which had been set to the liquid might be further scattered. When ignited the flames otherwise confined sought the easiest point of escape through these tubes.

Upon the deck four large barrels with spouts pointing upward, containing a similar liquid, performed a like function. The idea was to manœuvre such a vessel so that when abandoned it would float against an enemy ship and so ignite it. Naturally such a course was possible only in a general engagement. Ships specially constructed for this purpose were used in England until about the middle of the 18th Century, and until their devotion to this final sacrifice these vessels were used as guardships and for similar purposes. Later on it was found expedient to equip otherwise useless vessels for this certain destruction.

The peculiar form of the ports and the deck tubes may be seen in the illustration. What a terrifying sight these old fire ships must have presented; their sides spouting flames, mingled with the crash of exploding bombs, while from the deck apparatus jets sought the upper rigging and spars of any unfortunate ship which could not be manœuvred out of their way!

The Pink

THE PINK

THE word "pink" is another instance of a name applied to several quite different kinds of hulls and rigs at different epochs. The origin of the pink, like that of so many of the old types of vessels, is lost in the mists of the past. To a certain extent, naval archæology is like palæontology. Here and there, literally dug up by the student of marine science like fossil bones buried in the clays and drift of remote ages, are found representations of these old ships, and it is the work of many days and many minds to piece together these bits of evidence of the past, to assign to them their family, class, and specie, and eventually to reconstruct their entire origin and development. As often happens with fossil remains, many links are missing, so that we can only speculate as to how certain types came into being.

The upper portion of the pink's stern was drawn out more or less behind the body of the vessel proper and usually terminated in a much restricted quadrilateral transom. Below, the planking curved sharply to the stern post. This form of stern gave rise to the expression "pink-sterned." A hull having this form of stern was not necessarily a pink, but without it, the vessel certainly was not a pink.

However diversely the name may have been applied, Lescallier, edition of *l'an VI* (1795), gives a definite representation of a vessel bearing the name with the following concrete verbal description: "Pinque (pink) Mediterranean merchant vessel having two masts à calcet (i. e., with the galley form of masthead[1]). And on each one of them an antenna or lateen yard, with a very small mizzen away aft. This vessel resembles, in its rigging, a xebec with lateen sails. But the hull is different in that the pink has a much less straight sheer, its bow is fuller and its underbody less fine, being constructed to carry merchandise. Besides, the pinks are not propelled by oars and rarely carry cannon." He adds that the Spaniards and Neapolitans in their merchant marine employ many pinks, their size ranging from two hundred to three hundred tons. While he does not mention the characteristic stern, his picture shows it plainly enough.

Other representations said to be also of pinks show them as differing entirely from the above-quoted description.

The mists of the past shape themselves into definite forms. Emerging like clouds, these old ships, themselves larger or smaller clouds of sunlit canvas, when the broad light of efficient and naturalistic artists in clear-cut fashion limn their shapes for us, sail on, slowly or swiftly, as their destiny bears them, passing again into the obscurity of oblivion over the changeless ocean of time that knows them no more.

[1]See Note 8, Appendix.

The Patache

THE PATACHE

THE patache was another south European vessel now practically extinct. Baugean said in the year 1826 that the type was then dying out. It was a close relation of the vessel we would to-day call a brigantine, and belonged to that family of two-masted craft combining the square and the fore-and-aft rigs whose ancestry we have indicated in the articles dealing with the buss, the brig, and the snow. The foremast consisted of the conventional three sections, of lower mast, topmast, and top gallant each crossed with square yards. The mainmast was a single pole without topmast, supported by four shrouds on a side without ratlines as there was little occasion for going aloft on this spar. It bore a fore and aft gaff mainsail hooped to the mast, without a boom. This sail was hoisted and lowered by halyards and had no brails. The braces of the fore yard and topsail led to the foremost of the main strouds, while the topgallant braces led to the mainmast head. The bowsprit carried the customary jib, while of the two stays starting from the mainmast head, one led to the knight head and the other to the fore topmast head. Liberal staysails were carried on these stays.

The hull was cumbersome and heavy, terminating in a rounded stern pierced with small cabin windows.

These vessels, notoriously slow sailers, were commonly

employed in the coasting trade, more particularly in *le grand cabotage,* a rather vague term employed by the French to signify ocean voyages made without losing sight of the coasts of France, Spain, Holland, Portugal, and England, from the Strait of Gibraltar to the Channel. In the Mediterranean the term had a slightly different meaning and applied to voyages which did not pass beyond the Strait.

It was used in comparison with *le petit cabotage.* This term signified the carrying of cargoes in small boats from port to port without going out of the country of their origin, and always within a limited district.

These terms correspond somewhat to our own words interstate and intrastate commerce, but it is certain that there were, in the days of the patache, no such limitations upon its trade as have been placed by our Federal laws and Courts upon our variety of *grand cabotage.*

The Polacre

THE POLACRE

This is primarily a Mediterranean form of vessel. Its sharp bow has caused M. Jal to suggest that this feature is responsible for its name. This he derived from two Greek words Πολυ, much, and Ακρα, pointed.

The rig is also of Mediterranean origin and still exists. It was employed in England as late as fifty years ago. Its peculiarities were that usually it carried three pole masts without caps or crosstrees and a bowsprit consisting of one piece. Cleats were employed upon the masts as stops for the shrouds and stays. Sometimes the mizzen was not in one piece. The rigging was light, as there were no topmast shrouds or backstays—only stays on the upper part of the mast above the hoist of the topgallant. A survival from very early times was the Jacob's ladder on the after side of the mast, connecting the gap between the ending of the shrouds and the masthead.

Square courses, topsails, and topgallant sails garnished the fore and main masts, as well as, in early time, a lateen mizzen and square mizzen topsail.

Eighteenth-century polacres carried spritsails like ships.

The upper yards were devoid of horses or foot ropes because the men in furling or loosing the topsails stood upon the lower yards and upon the topsail yards to perform like offices for the topgallants, because this form of rig permitted the upper yards to come down the masts and to be assembled close together.

As usual, there were variations of the rig. Sometimes the topgallant mast was in a separate piece with the customary crosstrees.

Another closely related rig, according to Steele, was the polacre-settee, having a lateen foremast, like the xebec, and sometimes a lateen sail on the mizzenmast, the mainmast alone having square sails carried in true polacre fashion. This is probably the same rig called by Jal a polacre corvette. It is interesting to note that Lescallier's illustration of a polacre shows the mizzenmast in two pieces with a conventional round top. Brigs and barks were sometimes equipped in this fashion, but they were not true polacres.

Extensive inquiry among old-time local ship captains has failed to disclose any evidence that this type was ever employed or even seen on this side of the Atlantic within the last sixty years, although several stated that they were familiar with the polacres of French, Italian, Austrian, and Greek waters.

The Xebec

THE XEBEC

NEARLY everyone has, at a tender age, read "Robinson Crusoe." So that no one need confess that he or she is not acquainted with the word "xebec," connected with that hero's early adventure when he was a slave upon the north African coast.

The word is of eastern provenance and appears in many different forms both in Oriental countries and in those of the Romance languages. In as many forms also appears or appeared the hull and rig. Mr. B. Glanville Carney says that the xebec is a genus unto itself, but that it comprises several species and many types. In hull it is closely related to the galley, being rather narrow, with a prominent beak, and terminated aft with an outer platform comprised of two wings, the prolongations of the quarter gunwales or sides such as we have noted in several Mediterranean vessels related to the galley type.

The masts, three in number, usually bore lateen sails, the foremast having quite a pronounced rake forward. There were, however, many variations of the rig, because these vessels were often ship rigged, again like polacres, and yet again carried combinations of square and fore and aft sails. Naturally, oars were employed as a supplementary means of propulsion. The illustration shows a xebec as given by

Lescallier in his *Vocabulaire* published in the year 1777. It will be seen that the two forward masts consist of single poles *à calcet* while the mizzen consists of two parts with a small top and separate topmast.

The British Navy did not disdain to include this form of craft within its programme of construction. Two sloops, the *Dart* and the *Arrow*, built in 1796, were xebec shaped, without, however, some of the extreme features, such as the open overhang aft. They had narrow floors, considerable overhang forward and aft, and no "tumble-home." They were ship rigged, and while they appear to have distinguished themselves, the type was not repeated. Mr. Carney points out that this type was not a true xebec but rather a first cousin called the chambequin.

It is interesting to note that the English seamen called the lateen yard carried on the mizzen a "shebeck" yard, probably because that approximated the pronunciation of the French word for "xebec" and "chabek," and because the use of the lateen mizzen was retained longer in the French than in the English Navy.[1]

[1] See Note 8, Appendix.

The Saïque

THE SAÏQUE

THE notions of many persons as to the appearance of the vessels of the Levant are necessarily vague. We like to think of the craft of the Near East as possessing strange lines of hull and *bizarrerie* of rig. But in this the facts will not bear us out. Even in the earliest times concerning which we have fairly reliable information, that is from the latter part of the 16th Century, the shipping of the eastern part of the Mediterranean Sea did not differ greatly from the more western portions.

We seem to be reasonably certain that during the 16th Century the fore and aft sail, although in use in some of the north European countries had not penetrated into the Mediterranean. The lateen sail was characteristic of that region, but the square sail was also extensively employed. Mr. Nance says that the two typical vessels of Turkey during the 17th Century were the caramousel and saïque or saïc. They were more or less similar both in rigging and hull, except that the former had a much higher stern. The saïque was then a small sailing boat having a considerable sheer, with narrow wales and flat stern, rigged as shown in our illustration.

Some of the peculiarities of the rig may be noted, especially its three-capped topmast similar to that of the later polacre rigged vessels. The lateen mizzen is shown outside of the mizzen shrouds, but as it was a small sail it could be conveniently handled and easily changed over as occasion demanded.

The spritsail, it will be noticed, has the round holes in the lower corner designed to let out any water caught in the hollows of this piece of canvas, as it frequently dipped into the briny waves; so often, in fact, that it was sometimes called, not ineptly, the water sail.

Mr. Nance also says that the caramousel was probably extinct by the middle of the 18th Century but that the saïque was then still going strong with substantially the same rig, about which there certainly is nothing particularly Oriental looking.

Counterparts may be found for practically all the gear in northern ships of the period.

All this goes to prove that both the differences of rig in various parts of Europe in vessels of comparatively similar types, and the changes developed therein during several centuries, are much less than might at first be supposed.

A Capital Ship of 1820

A CAPITAL SHIP OF 1820

No BOOK about old ships, particularly none that would make a point of emphasizing the romance of ancient shipping, could justifiably omit Nelson's *Victory.*

Not only was Horatio, Lord Nelson one of the most romantic figures in the history of the English-speaking peoples, but the ship identified with his crowning success and death at the moment of triumph, the *Victory,* is the epitome of all that is inspiring and romantic in marine lore.

Nelson's *Victory* was the fifth ship in the British Navy to bear that name. The first *Victory* began her career as a merchant ship under the name of the *Christopher.* Just when she was built is not known but apparently she was purchased for the Royal Navy in the year 1562, and renamed. The three following *Victories* were launched in the years 1620, 1675, and 1737 respectively.

Nelson's *Victory* was launched in 1765. She cost originally £63,000. Since then (for nearly everyone knows that she is still in existence) she has had numerous rebuildings and repairs, until her total cost to the British nation has now reached the astonishing figure of upward of £500,000. But as a national asset she is worth every penny of her cost.

Nelson took command of the *Victory* in May, 1803. At that time the appearance of her hull, as it was when she was launched, had been considerably changed during her reconstruction in 1800 after the battle of Cape St. Vincent in 1797.

As to rigging of course the earlier vertical sprit topmast had been replaced by a jib-boom, a martingale helped to support the bowsprit, trail boards gave more protection to the beak-head, the long lateen yard on the mizzenmast had disappeared, and various small modifications, rather in application than in principle, rendered the rigging more efficacious.

The rebuilding of 1814–16 again changed the appearance of the *Victory's* hull to that which it bears to-day and such as we show it. Efforts are now being made in England to raise money by private subscription to restore the grand old vessel to the form she bore when she fought at Trafalgar. Nelson's immortal exhortation, "England expects every man to do his duty" (with the substitution of the proper country for the word "England") might well serve as a motto for us of to-day, when nearly all nations are suffering under a decided loss of spirituality.

It is a strange commentary upon the times that the World War brought forth no one outstanding figure in any country, with perhaps a single exception, Italy, that evoked demonstrations of popularity and devotion to compare with those which were evoked by Nelson.

A Frigate of 1820

A FRIGATE OF 1820

WHEN we come to compare the frigate of the first quarter of the 19th Century with earlier examples of the same type, we find that, while there has been some development in the rigging, not much change has occurred in the hull during the period of about thirty years.

Trail boards, that is, solid construction, enclosed the old-fashioned open beak-head, thus providing additional protection to the forecastle bulkhead. The open space, formerly to be found between the bulwarks of the foredeck and after-deck, that is, opposite what might be called the waist, if frigates can truly be said to have waists (the example of the fashionable young women of to-day may be noted) was solidly built up with a permanent structure except for a single narrow opening on each side for access to the deck. Boat davits had appeared at the quarters.

In the rigging it may be noticed that the fashion at this date was for extremely long jib-booms and flying jib-booms, thus creating an immense forward triangle within which to set a steadily increasing number of jibs. The bowsprit and its extensions were supported by a most elaborate forked martingale, and its whole structure was strengthened by additional rigging made possible by the elimination of the spritsail and the spritsail topsail. The old spritsail yard was still retained as a means of further strengthening the bowsprit in the horizontal plane.

Royals were a part of the regular equipment and not occasional sails, set temporarily upon a long-poled topgallant mast. Extra crosstrees and shrouds added further security for the royals upon the royal mast, while an additional pole set abaft this spar furnished a convenient medium for setting sky sails.

Altogether, the light weather sail spread had increased, still further heightening the dignity of these beautiful fabrics, approaching, at this period, the zenith of their grace and majesty.

The frigates were the eyes of the fleets of which they formed part, the scout-cruisers of their day. Also they were of the greatest service as commerce destroyers, running down (we came near saying "to earth") the proverbially timid merchant ship if not strongly convoyed.

What stories are more thrilling with adventurous romance than those of the frigates of this period whose exploits are so near our own times that none of the essence or flavour of the tales escapes us!

It is worth noting that in France, the custom had been to give to the frigates names of a feminine gender, such as *La Victoire, La Gloire*, etc., while to larger ships, names of the opposite sex were usually applied. We will leave it to our readers of the fair sex to determine whether this was due to the saucier and more jaunty appearance of the frigates when compared with the cumbersome but perhaps more majestic impression created by the craft of greater tonnage.

The Brig

THE BRIG

THE origin of this type of rig has been variously assigned by students of the evolution of sailing craft. Some would trace its ancestry to a late 16th Century two-masted vessel similar in rig to the buss, or to the buss itself. Others claim that the early brigantine with a fore and aft mainsail was the progenitor of the brig and that the word "brig" is merely a shortening of that longer appellation. Others prefer to think that the brig is an adaptation of a three-masted ship, the mizzenmast being omitted. Whatever may have been their origin, the three terms, snow, brigantine, and brig seem at various periods to have been much confused and applied rather indiscriminately to three kinds of vessels between which we to-day would not hesitate to differentiate.

If the brig be compared with a ship deprived of its mizzenmast, we shall note some differences.

In a ship the main braces lead aft to the extreme limit of the quarter. This method is obviously more or less inapplicable to a brig, as such a lead tends to pull down upon the main yard when it is sharply braced. Although perhaps this was not always the method of leading them, the braces of the main yard as well as the main topsail yard and main topgallant sail yard lead forward. These forward main-yard braces correspond to the preventer main braces often employed in ships for hauling the weather side of the main yard forward, instead of placing the major part of the strain upon the leeward main brace.

Other peculiarities might formerly have been noted in that brigs during the later years of the 18th Century rarely carried square main courses, their mainsails being of the fore-and-aft character, usually with a boom, the forward side or luff of the sail being attached to the after side of the main-mast by means of hoops sliding upon the mainmast. Such a brig carried a cross jack yard instead of a main yard. These characteristics differentiated the brig from the snow (*q. v.*) which carried a square mainsail in addition to its fore and aft mainsail, the latter normally rigged upon a try-sail mast. Man-of-war brigs sometimes were fitted with a "horse," that is, a vertical rope to which the luff of the fore and aft mizzen was fastened by hanks in the same manner as a stay-sail or jib. Brigs to-day are often fitted with a square mainsail in addition to their fore and aft mainsail, just as ships now usually carry square mizzen courses on their cross-jack yards. Brigs are very handy and many of them sail fast. They were a favourite medium of privateering, and it was a short step from that occupation to piracy. And the brig was what might have been termed the pirate's own vessel.

About a hundred years ago brigs were much employed in sea-going commerce. From the many delightful pictures made by Mediterranean artists, the brothers Roux, Corneille, Pellegrini and others, it would seem as if one of the main events of the career of such a vessel, if not absolutely the most important, was to have its portrait painted at Marseilles or Genoa by one of these delightful and competent artists.

Owing to this custom, we have to-day many intimate and spirited representations of these vessels, with their names and those of their masters, information which gives the key to the history of much of the shipping of the period.

Besides their regular cargoes, our vessels often brought back mementoes and treasures for the dear ones at home, carved coral, mandarin coats, laces, fine Chinese and European porcelains, the latter commodity then practically at the height of its artistic excellence.

To judge by the fine examples of many of these works of art still in the possession of the descendants of America's early seamen, the old-time ship masters must have had almost as good a weather eye for the colour and decoration of a fine Derby or Spode tea-set or the delicate modulation and paste of a Kwang He vase, as for the indications of a coming favourable breeze or for bad weather.

One has only to visit the Essex Institute and the Peabody Museum in Salem, Massachusetts, to see many examples of these treasures and the delightful old-time portraits of the vessels which brought them to this country.

The Snow

THE SNOW

In our article upon the brig, we discuss its possible origin. What is there stated applies to a certain extent as well to the snow. Probably before the year 1600 the brig and the snow had a common ancestor in a type of small two-masted vessel. From the evidence at hand, as Mr. Alan Moore puts it, prior to the year 1700 we are, as to the pedigree of the snow, upon an uncharted sea.

A contemporary drawing of the year 1700 shows a two-masted square-rigged vessel with round tops but no trysail. It is designated a snow.

Steele's "Elements & Practice of Rigging & Seamanship" (1794) gives the following definition: "A snow is the largest two-masted vessel, and is extremely convenient for navigation. The sails and rigging on the fore and main mast are similar to those on the same mast in a ship, the braces of the sails on the mainmast leading forward: besides which, there is a small mast, close behind the mainmast, that carries a trysail, resembling the mizzen of a ship. This mast, called the trysail mast, is fixed in a step of wood on deck, and the head fixed by an iron clamp on the aftside of the main top."

In his accompanying illustration, he shows a vessel with a large square mainsail set upon a formidable main yard, with a fore and aft trysail set with a gaff but with no boom, and attached with hoops to the trysail mast.

His pendant view of a brig shows the fore and aft mainsail with boom and gaff set on hoops on the mainmast, and a thin cross-jack yard bare of any sail.

Steele continues, "An Hermaphrodite is a vessel so constructed as to be occasionally a snow and sometimes a brig. It has two mainsails, a boom mainsail when a brig, and a square mainsail when a snow; and a main topsail larger than the fore topsail. Sometimes the boom mainsail is bent to the mainmast, as a brig or on a trysail mast, as a snow." He gives no view of this hybrid nor does he mention the brigantine.

Many persons insist on calling brigantines hermaphrodite brigs. It seems to be more difficult, however, to distinguish between the brigs and snows, as both partook and still partake of the same peculiarities of rig. The claim has been made also, that the trysail mast is not or was not originally the distinguishing feature of the snow; and that it was, rather, the shape of the hull at the bow which gave it the name (snausnout).

Our illustration shows the good old-fashioned snow of Steele's time, with trysail mast, quarter galleries, and bewindowed stern, capacious lanterns, plenty of sheer and tumble-home; without doubt "extremely convenient for navigation."

The Brigantine

THE BRIGANTINE

In DEALING with this subject, it is essential, as Mr. R. C. Anderson says, to define the date as well as the nationality of the vessel under consideration. Probably the name has been applied at various times to many vessels differing altogether in hull and rig.

Naval archæologists have been long striving to trace the origin and descent of this form of rig, but every new contribution to the subject seems to complicate the matter still further. Many writers have used the word "brig" as a contraction of "brigantine."

Leaving aside all puzzling attempts to arrive at any conclusions based upon etymology, or upon the divergences of local applications of the name, it seems safe to assume that as early as 1692 there was in northern waters a well-defined type of two-masted vessel probably carrying a fore and aft sail upon a buss form of mainmast, that is, one without a round top. The form of the foremast seems to be in doubt. At all events, it was square rigged.

A distinctive feature of the later 17th and 18th Century brigantine with its mainmast, formed of a rather lofty lower spar and a topmast, joined with a crosstree and not with a round or partly curved top, such as its foremast carried.

The forward mast was regularly ship rigged with course,

topsail, and top gallant. The brigantines of about the year 1750 usually carried at least one square sail on its main topmast. At a later period the size of the square sails upon the main topmast tended to diminish until ultimately these disappeared altogether and the gaff topsail took their place.

There have been besides several variations of this rig, nominally described as schooner-brigs and brig-schooners; formerly, in England or America, they would probably have been called brigantines.

A salient feature of the early brigantine and one which no doubt gives us a clue to the reason for the application of the name to the type of vessel we have been considering, was that many of them were equipped with oars. Not being very large, they could be thus propelled in and out of harbours against head winds and also at sea when the weather was calm. The existence of several contemporary models serves to confirm this view.

The pictures labelled brigantines by Lescallier (1777) and Falconer (1815) certainly look more like brigs. Steele omits all mention of this type. We prefer to think of the brigantine as more like the vessel called a brig-schooner by Baugean in his *"Collection de toutes Espèces de Batiments,"* and believe that she is the kind of vessel described by James Fenimore Cooper and called "le Feu Follet."

The Ship "Felicity"

EXTRACTS FROM THE LOG OF THE SHIP "FELICITY"

WEST INDIAMAN, OF TRURO,
ROBERT OAKAPPLE, MASTER

June 3rd, 1820—Going down to the vessel for launching at 10:30 A. M. met woman with empty pail and passed the Rev. Adam Noble. Launching unsuccessful. Ways broke down. Fear the hull has been strained.

June 16th—Hull jacked up and ways repaired. Builder reports no injury to vessel. Ship took the water at 12:15 P. M.

June 30th—Great difficulty in securing crew to take vessel around to London.

* * * * *

July 10th—Weighed anchor 5:20 A. M., stood down channel under all plain sail. Temperature 62. Wind light S. S. W. Fair, Glass steady, 29.51.

July 12th—Mate reports that seaman had brought one of those furry things[1] on board in a covered cage. Ordered its neck wrung and body thrown overboard. Story of launching has gotten about. Crew grumbling, wish me to turn back. Temperature 70. Wind steady S. E. fair.

* * * * *

[1]See Note 9, Appendix.

July 26th—St. Elmo's fire on yards and trucks lasted fifteen minutes. Strange spectacle. Lat. N. 31.35, Long. W. 41.13. Temperature 71. Wind N. E. Cloudy.

July 27th—Yesterday fell in with large topsail schooner; thought it to be a slaver. Came within hail and stated he was short of water; asked if I could give him some; long boat came alongside about 7:30 P. M. and seven men came on deck. Drew pistols, backed me into cabin, bound me, took what money I had, water and other things they wanted, compelled six of crew to accompany them, leaving the rest bound, and vessel hove to. In no condition to resist. Mate managed to free himself and others. Now short handed. Temperature 69. Wind N. E. strong, fair.

August 6th—Two of crew sick, think slavers men brought small pox on board. Wind N. E. by N. Lat. N. 25.07, lon, W. 52.22 W. Temperature 72. Moderate, fair.

August 7th—Another man down. Occasional showers. Temperature 65. Wind N. E., cloudy.

August 8th—Curious sunset last night; whole sky orange coloured. Wind baffling and puffy; glass falling. Now under reefed topsails. Temperature 78. Wind N. E., cloudy.

August 9th—Dismasted. Sudden squall of hurricane force from S. E. for about six minutes. Too short handed to reduce sail quick enough. Long boat crushed by fall of foremast, lost two men overboard. Ship leaking badly; clear water coming up from pumps. Temperature 74. Wind now light, N. E., fair, no observation to-day.

August 11th—Balance of sound hands left ship in jolly boat while I was in hold with carpenter trying to locate leak. Ship sinking. One of sick died last night. God help us.

*   *   *   *   *

(A half cask, containing the log-book from which the foregoing extracts are taken, was picked up by the bark *Emilia* of Fair Haven, Mass., on August 12, 1820, in N. latitude 23°59′, longitude W. 51°41′.)

The Corvette

THE CORVETTE

THE word "corvette" seems a hard etymological nut to crack.

Jal and some of his followers claim its derivation from the latin *corbis* meaning a peculiar form of Roman basket as applied to the Roman merchant ships called *corbitæ*. (Compare Roman *corbita*, page 50.)

Kenna denies this derivation and contends that the word is of Netherlandish origin; that its earliest known appearance is in 1476 and that if it were derived from Mediterranean sea language, it should be possible to find some connecting link and transitional stage between Roman times and the 15th Century. He says that the word occurs first and most frequently in parts of Flanders near the French border and that about the year 1500 there was a type of Dutch fishing boat similar to a dogger then called a *cobre* and later *corve*.

The divergence of form of the craft to which the word "corvette" has been applied is almost as confusing as the origin of the word itself. We have seen that it was first used for a boat like a dogger. In the 17th Century the corvette is described as a sort of *barque longue* having only one mast and a little stay-sail and propelled by both sails and oars. The definition of a *barque longue*, which it is unnecessary to quote, still further complicates the matter. In the early years of the 18th Century, corvettes are described as having two masts and a bowsprit carrying a spritsail. After the middle of that century Jal states that the corvette had increased in size and had taken a form similar to that of a ship of the time. He describes the corvette of his day (1840) as having the general build of a frigate with similar masts and sails, and mounting from 14 to 32 guns.

As usually understood, the corvette was a name common in the French Navy and applied to that class of smaller war vessels somewhat analogous to the ships called, in the British and American navies, sloops of war. Hamersly's "Naval Encyclopædia" says that the term was never adopted in the United States Navy.

Corvettes were distinguished by their comparatively low freeboard and absence of a high quarterdeck.

Corvette is a fascinating word. One would like to derive it from *corbeau*, a raven, and to imagine the commander of such a vessel as displaying a red flag showing a raven in full flight holding a skull in its claws, with the motto *Gare le corbeau*, reminiscent of the wicked Templar in that favourite romance of our boyhood days, "Ivanhoe."

The Topsail Schooner

THE TOPSAIL SCHOONER

JUST why this term should be applied to schooners carrying square yards and square topsails is not apparent. A far greater number of schooners, particularly in America, carry topsails than those which have none, but to-day nearly all of these employ topsails of the gaff variety—not square topsails.

In his excellent note upon "The Origin of the Schooner Rig,"[1] Mr. L. G. Carr-Laughton, the Librarian of the British Admiralty, says that the essentials of the schooner rig are two gaff sails and a headsail, all beyond is accidental. He also says that embryonic schooners without a headsail were being used in Holland as early as 1630.

One of the earliest representations of a true schooner is to be found in Richard Houston's engraving of " A Fresh Gale," after W. Van de Velde, and although an exact date cannot be assigned to the painting it is reasonable to assign the picture, and consequently the schooner, to the last quarter of the 17th Century.

In early times, the popular rig for yachts was that of the hoy, whose rig often included a square topsail. It was quite natural therefore that this feature should be embodied in the rig of the schooner where, upon the foremast, such a form of sail would be equally efficacious.

[1] *Mariner's Mirror*, vol. 1, no. 1, p. 28.

Mr. C. G. 't Hooft has written charmingly in the *Mariner's Mirror* for October, 1919, of the early English yachts, the first of which was of Dutch provenance. His article contains much historical information upon the subject, many quaint excerpts from Samuel Pepys' diary anent these pleasure craft of royalty, and considerable romance relating to the command of these little vessels by their princely skippers, with descriptions of their rich fittings and decorations and of the early days of the noble sport of yacht racing.

The Goëlette

THE GOËLETTE

It is sometimes difficult to differentiate between closely related types of vessels and perhaps no fine distinction need be drawn between the rig called by the French a *goëlette* and that which we commonly designate as a schooner.

However, the goëlette often presents interesting variations not seen in our western fore and aft schooners.

Notwithstanding the Dutch sound of the name, Jal attributes an American origin to the word *schooner* and also to the rig. Perhaps he too had heard the Gloucester tale of the origin of the schooner (*q. v.* infra.) He says he cannot trace the vessel's construction earlier than the 18th Century, although he admits that its origin may have a greater antiquity.

The derivation of the French word is interesting, coming apparently from the word *gwelon* (*goëlan*), employed by the Bretons to designate the sea gull in allusion to its melancholy cry (*givella*=Celto-Breton, to weep). Probably the peaked sails of the two-masted goëlette, especially when set wing and wing, suggested to the poetically inclined minds of the Bretons the suddenly upraised wings of the goëlan in the act of making the first stroke of its pinions when rising in flight from the sea.

The name seems to have been applied in the Mediterranean to the schooner rig (with certain attributes peculiar to the locality) on account of its trapezoidal sails.

Jal's description fits our American schooners pretty well, at least those of his day, as he mentions that the masts have a decided rake aft. It will be remembered that it was formerly the custom so to incline the masts of nearly all our vessels.

One of the variations of the goëlette rig that may be mentioned is the employment of a trysails mast *before* the foremast. Two square yards are rigged upon this, the lower one fixed and the upper one susceptible of being hoisted and lowered above it. Mr. H. S. Vaughan has suggested that this is a survival of a feature of the polacca rig. Such a trysail mast, with its yards, is removable and may be lowered and stowed away. The braces of the upper yard are single, the lower rove with a pendant and whip, both leading through rings attached by tricing lines to the main rigging, the hauling parts leading to the quarter.

As to the origin of the word "schooner" as signifying a vessel of the type above described, nearly everyone is familiar with the tale of the launching of the new type of vessel at Andrew Robinson's yard at Gloucester, Mass., in the year 1713, where, as the vessel left the ways, a bystander exclaimed, "See how she scoons!" Upon which Robinson is reported to have said, "A schooner let her be!" The difficulty with this yarn is that "the new type of vessel" was at that date not a new type of vessel at all. Mr. Carr Laughton suggests that the Gloucester vessel was of the newer and finer design of hull which at about the period of the alleged Robinson incident came to be associated with the rig now called a schooner, and that it was to the hull and not to the rig that the word was applied.

The word "schooner" cannot be traced before 1713, nor, despite its sound, can it be assigned to a Dutch origin. (Compare the article on the goëlette.)

The square topsails were probably acquired by the schooner at an early date for the reason that the rig was associated with the early normal yacht hull. Square sails were largely employed upon the early yachts, for it must be borne in mind that, despite the application to-day of the term "yacht" to any sort of pleasure craft, originally it had a meaning restricted to a particular type of hull and rig.

The Packet Ship

THE PACKET SHIP

AFTER the close of the War of 1812, the renewal of commercial relations between the United States and England demanded increased shipping facilities. To supply this demand, beginning about the year 1816, numerous lines of packet ships came into being.

The packets, ranging from 300 to 500 tons register, were flush-decked, full-bodied vessels. The only permanent structure above deck was a caboose or galley. It was the fashion at first to paint the hulls of these ships black above the water line with bright varnished upper works, while the inside of the bulwarks, galley, etc., was coloured green. The size of the packet ship gradually increased until, at the time they were supplanted by the clippers, many were over 1,000 tons, while one registered as much as 1,439 tons.

About the year 1830 the poop deck made its reappearance as a feature of the packets. This structure was given over almost entirely to passenger cabins and immediately became popular. Following this innovation, deck houses were also added, while a topgallant forecastle, small at first, gradually was increased in size until it reached back as far as the main hatch. The fashion in painting also changed. A broad white band, broken by black squares in imitation of the gun port of a warship, was a favourite style, while the inside work was painted in some light colour instead of green.

The packet ships carried plenty of sail—studding sails on all the yardarms up to the topgallant, except on the mizzen. Skysails for summer use were set on removable polemasts above the royals. Even under favourable conditions these vessels could not sail much faster than twelve knots on the average, yet so hard were they driven that voyages from New York to Liverpool in sixteen days were not uncommon, while occasionally a trip was made inside of two weeks.

The firms owning packet lines had their distinctive emblems, many painted on the sails—another renewal of an old-time sea custom.

Interesting anecdotes are related about these packet ferries. A favourite yarn slyly circulated by the crew among the ignorant steerage passengers was to the effect that if the weather became bad, the captain would blow a whistle and the ship would be cut in half, the forward part proceeding without the aftermost portion. This appalling possibility kept many a credulous voyager awake night after night, and drove many to sleep unprotected on the forward deck rather than risk being left behind.

Irish emigration was at its height during the period of the packet ships, and many were the romances both ended and begun when Paddy or Terrence shouldered his bundle, stepped aboard the packet, and was "off for Philadelphia in the mornin'."

A New Bedford Whaling Bark

A NEW BEDFORD WHALING BARK

"THAR she blows! An' sparm at that!" comes from the crow's nest high up on the foremast. "Where away?" " 'Bout three p'ints off the port bow." Instantly the vessel's deck teems with activity. The "Old Man," as the captain is usually called, bustles up through the after companion hatch. The bark has been out of luck so far this voyage, and this is the first school sighted. The tumult increases, but it is an orderly tumult, where every man knows and does exactly what is required of him. Boats must be hoisted out, the vessel's course altered, yards braced; sheets, tacks, and bowlines handled; sail spread or shortened as occasion demands; stages rigged, fires lighted, a multiplicity of acts performed.

Meanwhile, the boats have got off, and, urged along by sturdy muscles, approach the quarry. And it is exactly in this respect—the rapidity and facility with which the boats could be put overboard—that the whalers contributed a most useful appliance to marine science.

In olden times the hoisting in and out of a boat was a comparatively complicated and tedious operation. It was performed by means of several tackles. In taking a boat on board, first the yard tackles hanging from pendants at the arms of the fore and main yards lifted the boat from the water high enough to clear the rail; then by means of other tackles and guys, the boat was directed over its chocks, to which it was lowered and secured.

About the end of the 18th Century the earliest form of boat davit made its appearance. It consisted of a long stout beam extending across the extreme end of the hull on both sides of the stern for a considerable distance beyond the vessel's sides. Forward of this and right aft of the mizzen shrouds a stout, removable, vertical stanchion was fitted. To the top of this and from the end of the cross beam, tackles were rigged and these lifted the boat diagonally to the line of the ship's keel, thus easily clearing the spread of the quarter gallery. In this position the boat was readily secured and was in position for immediate lowering.

It was a simple and obvious progression from this to the conventional outboard davit. The end of the above-mentioned cross beam also furnished a convenient point to which to attach the after block of main braces, and it was for this purpose that this cross beam continued to be used long after its original purpose as a part of the quarter davit had disappeared.

Another peculiarity of the whaling vessels of the United States is their two narrow raised deck houses astern. The convenience of these is obvious.

The bark rig was a favourite one with the whaler as it afforded an opportunity to keep all the main braces aloft and thus out of the way of the continually handled boats, while the fore and aft mizzen had conspicuous advantages when it came to lying-to.

Apparently the rig was evolved about the end of the 18th

or the beginning of the 19th Century. Darcy Lever (1808) mentions that it was customary for vessels in the Baltic trade to substitute a flagstaff for the mizzen topmast, its top yards and gear, and to omit also the cross-jack yard, retaining only the driver, a fore and aft sail, on the mizzenmast. This would leave the vessel substantially bark-rigged. Subsequent development substituted a more elaborate spar for the flagstaff, one capable of carrying a gaff topsail, and the type was complete.

There is plenty of romance in whaling, when seen from a landsman's eyes, but there could not have been much romance in the minds of men who pursued this calling. The chase, harpooning, and lancing of the huge quarry had its wild thrills, but the following acts of the drama, the stripping and hoisting in of the blubber and the trying out of the oil, were certainly fetid and repulsive anticlimaxes.

Although fortunes were rapidly acquired in the pursuit of the whale, particularly prior to the year 1860, after that date, the owners of the whaling ships often suffered severe reverses. The Civil War played havoc among the whalers of the northern ports. Many ships were captured by the cruisers of the Confederacy. Of these not a few were herded into Southern harbours and there deliberately sunk to improve the defenses of those havens.

Again in the winter of the year 1871, thirty-two whaling vessels were nipped in the Arctic ice and totally destroyed, the crews numbering more than 1,200 men barely escaping with their lives. This blow fell most heavily upon the city of New Bedford, Massachusetts.

The discovery of and enormous increase in the production of petroleum sounded the death knell of the whaling industry. And while the whale is still pursued, the harpoon gun, the bomb and steam whalers have superseded the hand-rowed boat, hand harpoon, and lance, and have also robbed the trade of such romance as it formerly had. These modern appliances have also almost exterminated the whale, and the day is not far off, unless a comprehensive international policy of conservation is agreed upon, adopted, and firmly enforced, when the cetaceans will become as scarce as the old-time whaling ships.

The Barquentine

THE BARQUENTINE

THE Dutch name for a vessel with a square-rigged fore-mast, with a mainmast devoid of square-rig features and carrying a fore and aft main sail, was a "barkentyne." Such a vessel might possibly now be called a brigantine, although the description given above is perhaps too vague to indicate clearly the exact form of the rig of such a vessel.

The barquentine of to-day is a vessel of three or more masts having a three-piece or ship's foremast (that is, one with a lower mast joined at the topmast with a "top" or plat-form, the topgallant mast being joined to the topmast with crosstrees), and with two or more fore-and-aft rigged masts following this form of foremast. A trysail is often employed upon the foremast, in which case a main-staysail would necessarily be omitted.

Just how and when this rig made its appearance has not yet been fully determined. It does not seem to have been in general use as early as the latter part of the 18th Century. Falconer (1771) does not mention it, nor Steele nor Baug-ean. Cooke's "Sixty-five Plates of Shipping" (1829) does not give a representation. The barquentine to-day is prob-ably to be found in greater numbers on the Pacific Ocean than elsewhere. The weather and wind conditions there seem to be particularly favourable to its survival. It is largely employed in the sugar trade between the western coast of the northern continent and the Hawaiian Islands. With long stretches of steady breezes and fair weather, the advantages of the schooner for close-hauled reaches are apparent, while with quartering gales the square-rigged foremast is a decided help.

There are many variations of rig intermediate between the brig and the schooner, and between the ship, the bark, and the barquentine. For instance, a brig might be found with a fore and aft sail on the foremast; this sail would be called a "benjamine." A schooner might be found to carry no fore and aft foresail and to have square sails of the foremast and a main-staysail. She would, nevertheless, be still a schooner provided the foremast was joined to the topmast by a crosstree or spreader.

These verbal distinctions may seem rather obscure to the landlubbers, but what is the use of a profession if it hasn't cryptic terminology?

The Clipper Ship of 1850

THE CLIPPER SHIP OF 1850

THE late Captain Arthur H. Clark, who probably knew as much as any one about American shipping, and about the clipper ship in particular, said that while the origin of the word "clipper" is not clear, it might be derived from the verb "clip," a term of many meanings as exemplified in the New England slang expression, "a fast clip." He then says that when vessels of a new model, intended to *clip* over the waves rather than to plough through them, were built, they became known as clippers. Be this as it may, it is certain that the fast Baltimore privateers and vessels engaging in the tea trade were known as clippers as early as 1810. The long, narrow hulls of these vessels, principally small craft, brigs, brigantines, and schooners, rarely exceeding two hundred tons, were patterned after the French luggers, which visited the United States in the latter part of the 18th Century.

The earliest clipper ship, according to Captain Clark, was the *Ann McKim* of 493 tons built in Baltimore in 1832. She was a larger edition of the earlier clipper brigs and schooners. The type was still further developed, particularly by the improvements made by John W. Griffiths of New York. In 1843, the *Rainbow,* a vessel of 750 tons, having a convex stem and rounded main transom, was constructed according to Mr. Griffiths's designs and proved a great success. Thereafter, large numbers of similar vessels were constructed, both in England and in the United States, the size gradually increasing until the average tonnage was well over one thousand, while such great ships as the *Sovereign of the Seas* of 2,421 tons and the *Great Republic* of 4,357 tons marked the zenith of the development of sailing craft.

These superb vessels, stoutly constructed, splendidly rigged, well manned, and ably officered, sailed every sea, carrying on through thick and thin, establishing records for speed almost equalling the steamships of to-day.

The *Flying Cloud* sailed 374 miles in twenty-four hours! This was on her famous trip from New York to San Francisco in eighty-nine days and twenty hours in the year 1851.

Those were the declining days of the romance of the sea. The sun of the sailing ship was setting. Already the gold and the crimson were mantling the skies—the gold of California and the crimson of the coming Civil War. But the glory of that sunset was the brighter by reason of the perfection to which the ingenuity of man had brought that most romantic of his handservants, the ship.

The Modern Super Ship
A Five-Masted Bark

THE MODERN SUPER SHIP
A FIVE-MASTED BARK

IF A full-rigged ship of, say, one hundred and twenty-five years ago, could be placed alongside a modern steel sailing ship of similar tonnage, it would be interesting to compare the many differences to be observed between the two.

Beginning with the hulls, it would be noted that at the bow, the later ship's stem was altogether dissimilar to that of her older sister. In the latter a straight cut-water or stem-piece, raking forward at an angle of about forty-five degrees, terminated in a figurehead set squarely and practically vertically upon it. The stem-piece was joined on each side to the forebody of the ship above the water line by three or more curving pieces of wood called rails of the head, these being again strengthened by vertical ties crossing the said rails at right angles and floored with several curved wooden gratings in the middle of which rose the bowsprit at a quite steep angle or "steeve." This whole structure was called the vessel's beak-head, and all of it was quite separate from the vessel's hull. At this point the hull itself was rounded while lower down near the water line the form still showed a convex curve. The modern bow would be concave at the water line, while on deck the lines would be almost straight and join at an acute angle right at the stem, entirely embracing

within the hull's structure all that part of the vessel formerly composing the beak-head. The transition may be traced
through the trail boards and the ultimate covering in of all
the open framing of the beak-head.

The figurehead has disappeared and in its place one may
notice at most a few gilt scrolls, or more likely no ornament
whatsoever. The steeve or inclination of the bowsprit has
decreased and has approached more nearly the horizontal.
Gone are the spritsail yard and spritsail topsail formerly
swung under the bowsprit and jib boom. In addition to the
bobstays and extending down from the bowsprit cap is a
truss for the lower bowsprit stays sometimes called a dolphin
striker.

The bowsprit shrouds, no longer needed as guys for the
support of the spritsail yard, now stretch from the vessel's
hull direct to their points of support upon the bowsprit
proper and jib boom. Even the successor of the spritsail
yard long used after the disappearance of the square headsail, as a spreader for the bowsprit shrouds, is rarely to be
seen. In fact, in the most modern vessels the jib boom has
disappeared.

In many of the more modern steel and iron ships, the forecastle raised above the vessel's upper deck still survives,
while a similar structure aft, successor to the old-fashioned
quarterdeck but much shorter, is now usually dubbed the
turtle back. In the midships sections of the two hulls, not so
much difference would appear, for the merchant ship of
the beginning of the 19th Century had a flat floor, a quick
turn at the bilge, and nearly perpendicular sides with not

nearly so much tumble-home as the warships of the period showed. In the stern of the more modern ship a marked difference would be apparent. One would look in vain for the quarter galleries and for the transom with its many windows and fancy "ginger-bread work," as the old salts delighted to call the ornate gilded carvings formerly to be found in rich profusion on these portions of the vessel's structure.

In place of all these, the modern ship would be found to have a rounded stern shaped underneath like a melon cut in half along its largest axis. The vessel's sides, too, show many differences. The old longitudinal wales have given place to long lines of rivet heads marking only the joining of large rectangular metal plates. The wide projecting chain wales with their chain plates and deadeyes are gone, and in their places are individual plates riveted to the vessel's side, each terminating with an eye to receive the turnbuckles for setting up the shrouds and stays instead of the old-fashioned deadeyes and lanyards.

Turning to the spars we find steel largely replacing wood, although some of the smaller and lighter members are still wooden. The tops are noticeably smaller, while the form of the crosstrees has altered. Steel and bronze have replaced the standing rigging and to a certain extent some of the running rigging. Those parts of the sheets upon which the wear comes, i. e., those passing through the sheeves let into the yardarms and through the quarter blocks, are of chain.

The change effected by the employment of steel rigging was almost revolutionary. Hempen cordage was subject to quick decay and, what was worse, stretched interminably.

It was no uncommon event for a ship's mainstay, a rope usually about nine inches in circumference, to stretch four feet in the course of a long voyage. This continued lengthening necessitated frequent adjustment and was a constant menace to the security of the masts. Steel wire standing rigging requires practically no attention and is almost unbreakable.

The metal trusses bearing the yards have obviated the need of all the old gear such as trusses and parrels, and by reason of their extension of the yards far out from the masts, have enabled the yards to be more closely braced when on the wind. Double or upper and lower topsails and topgallant sails render easier the tasks of stowing and reefing these formerly unwieldy canvases, while skysails are now almost always a part of the ship's regular equipment. In former days royals seem to have been regarded as only occasional sails.

The leads of many of the braces too have been changed, especially those of the fore yard and all of the topmast yards. These now lead to the sides of the ship instead of to the stays and shrouds, dispensing with many leading blocks and much friction in handling, thereby saving both labour and cordage.

The blocks are now nearly always steel-strapped or constructed entirely of metal. On many of the later ships, fore and aft sails have made their appearance upon both fore and main masts in addition to that on the mizzenmast.[1]

The internal arrangements are similarly changed. Many

[1] See Note 10, Appendix.

of the large sailing ships have power for handling the sails furnished by means of steam or internal combustion engines. The pumps are operated by power and the interior of the vessel is adequately heated.

Notwithstanding the many labour-saving devices and appliances for the comfort and sanitary condition of the crew, the life of the common sailor, although not so hard as formerly, is still no sinecure.

Our illustration shows the 20th Century clipper, the super ship. This remarkable sailing vessel, the *Kobenhavn,* is 390 feet long on deck and 420 feet over all. Her breadth is 49 feet or a ratio of only one to eight. The proportion of the hull therefore approximates that of the extremely narrow galleys of the Middle Ages. The ship's gross tonnage is 3,965 and her load displacement is 7,900 tons. She is equipped with a wireless apparatus, and her form of construction resembles the modern steam vessel in having a double bottom and many longitudinal and transverse watertight bulkheads. And yet this huge vessel can be operated by a crew all told, including officers, of only sixty-five men and boys.

She was built at Leith, Scotland, in 1921 by Messrs. Ramage and Ferguson.

Steam navigation and wireless communication have robbed the sea of much of its mystery, one of its greatest sources of romance. But who can look at a fine ship or bark with its free lifting head-sails swelling to leeward, its snugly braced yards with their symmetrical squares of billowing canvas cut into rotund patterns by the buntlines and leach lines, the taut staysails and the light lacery of the rigging outlined against a gleaming sky, the white bone at its forefoot and the shimmering water astern, without experiencing a thrill to remind one of the inherent beauty of the old-fashioned sailing ship, its glorious past and its dubious future?

FINIS

APPENDIX

APPENDIX

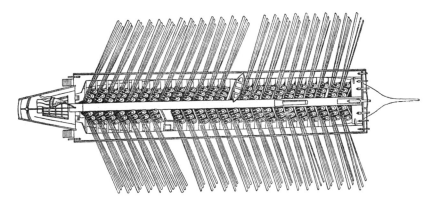

PLAN OF A GALLEY

A plane view of the arrangement of oars "à zenzile" in a galley of about the year 1400. It will be noted that on the starboard side, one bench of oars is omitted to afford space for the cook-stove and upon the port side, space is similarly left for the ship's boat. This illustration is taken from "Le Costruzioni Navali e L'Arte della Navigazione al Tempo di Cristoforo Columbo" by Enrico Alberto d'Albertis, 1893 (page 29).

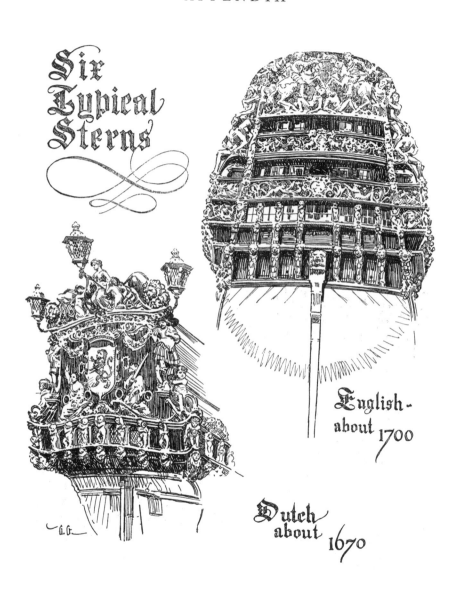

Six Typical Sterns

English about 1700

Dutch about 1670

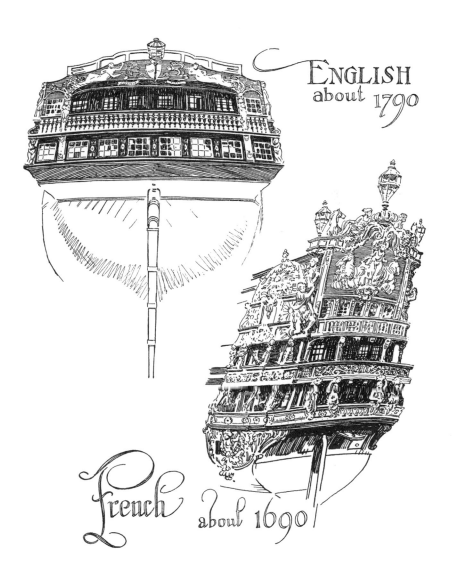

ENGLISH about 1790

FRENCH about 1690

AMERICAN
from FRENCH design
about 1797

Spanish
about
1800

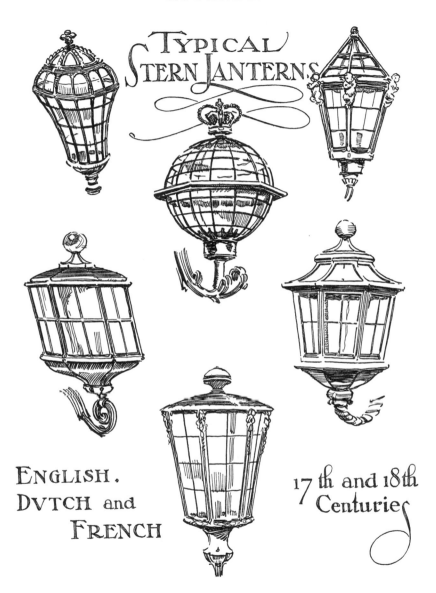

TYPICAL STERN LANTERNS

ENGLISH. DVTCH and FRENCH

17th and 18th Centuries

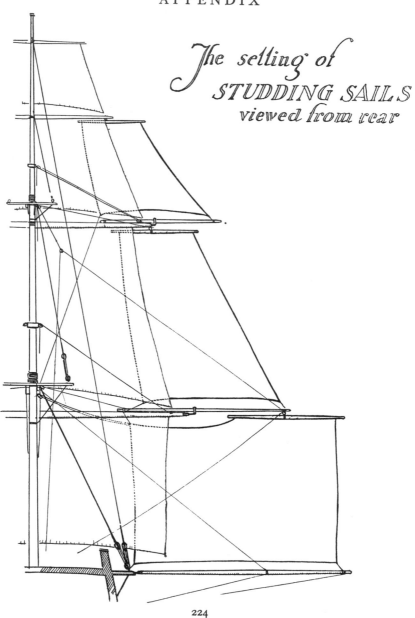

The setting of
STUDDING SAILS
viewed from rear

A 32 POUNDER
with its tackle and equipment

CANNON

A LIST of the names and sizes of the ordnance of antiquity includ-ing those most frequently employed upon vessels. The length of cannon was commonly referred to as the chace or chase.

Names	Chace		Size of Bore		Weight of Shot
Rabbinet	3	feet	1¾	inches	
Falconet	4	"	2	"	
Falcon	6	"	2¾	"	3 to 4 lbs.
Minion	8	"	3	"	5 to 6 "
Saker	9	"	3½	"	6 to 8 "
Demi-Culverin	10–12	"	4½	"	10 to 12 "
Culverin	11–13	"	5½	"	18 to 24 "
Demi-Cannon	10 to 12	"	6	"	about 36 "
Cannon	12	"	7	"	" 58 "
Long Culverin	16	"	4¾	"	12 to 15 "
Basalisk	20	"	4½	"	10 to 12 "

Until comparatively modern times ships hardly ever carried larger guns than demi-cannon.

APPENDIX

There were many smaller guns, frequently referred to as "murthering pieces," often set upon swivels, some breech-loading.

The sizes and weights given above are, of course, only approximate, as no fixed standard existed. Round stones were not infrequently fired instead of metal balls.

A typical Bow about 1830

LIKE all other engines employed upon sailing ships, the whipstaff was an evolution from the simple transverse tiller of early days. Immediately the changes wrought by moving the rudder from side to stern were accomplished, the erection of an after castle and its speedy enclosure, necessitated some means of placing the helmsman where he could have an unobstructed field of vision.

This was apparently accomplished not long after the above-mentioned change, perhaps as early as the middle of the 14th Century.

It is not known when the fulcrum for the upright lever was introduced, nor how early the pin at the end of the lever and the eye on the bottom of the upright staff employed in the French vessels were invented.

As the size of the ships increased and more decks were added, it was again necessary to find a method of providing an opening through which the helmsman could see.

At first a space was managed in the front of the poop. This sometimes took the form of a curved structure or arch (called in French the *dos d'âne*—ass's back) over the whipstaff. Still further increase in the size of the vessel again robbed the helmsman of his vision except for a little square scuttle over his head through which he could see the leaches of some of the sails and receive orders from the quartermaster conning the ship.

The inconvenience of this arrangement, nay, the danger arising from such a lack of vision, demanded the invention of a better appliance.

The whipstaff was a pretty poor affair. It did not permit the helm to be put hard over either side; consequently, as it could only be operated for a few degrees, much of the direction of a vessel's course was of necessity accomplished by the handling and trim of the sails. Moreover, it was stated that only one man could stand at the "whipp" conveniently. So that in large vessels and in foul weather this appliance could not be operated. Under such circumstances relieving tackles were placed upon the tiller. Some bright mind conceived the idea of placing the two ends of these tackles upon a drum, so that as one was wound in the other was let out. The steering wheel was the result—the most important advance in naval engineering in centuries. The exact date of its introduction is unknown but it is believed to have come into quite general use during the early years of the 18th Century.

NOTES

¶ (1) Page 10. *Parrels.* The parrel is a device still in use. Its purpose is to confine a spar or yard to the mast and yet permit the yard to turn freely with the mast as its axis and also to travel up and down that spar.

The earliest form of parrel was probably a rope loosely lashed about the mast and yard. At an early date this primitive method was improved upon by the construction of a parrel formed of short vertical battens of wood called sisters or ribs alternating with sets of wooden spheres called trucks, pieces of rope passing through holes driven transversely in the ribs and in the centres of the sisters, the ends of these ropes passing around the yard. The parrel usually consisted of three rows of trucks when used upon the courses or lower yards and of two such rows when used upon topsails. The topgallant, royal, staysail, and the spritsail yards were usually confined by rope parrels.

¶ 2. Page 48. *Greek Merchantman.* The datum from which the details concerning several of the repairs mentioned were taken, is to be found in the translation of a Jewish document of about 412 B. C. concerning the repairs of a boat of that date. This papyrus written

APPENDIX

in Aramaic, was recently discovered at Elephantine in the southern part of Egypt. For further reference see *Mariner's Mirror,* vol. IX, No. 7, p. 223 The original English source is No. 26 in "Jewish Documents of the Time of Ezra translated from the Aramaic," by A. Cowley, Bodley's Librarian, 1919.

¶ 3. Page 83. The *Great Harry.* Doubts have been raised that the *Great Harry* was present at Dover on the event of the embarkation of Henry VIII in May, 1521.

Consequently, the same suggestions would cast doubt upon the accuracy of the Hampton Court painting by Volpe alleged to depict that occurrence.

One of the main difficulties with the painting is that in the larger principal four-masted vessels shown (we would be inclined to say that they belonged to the carrack family) a square sail is shown upon the mizzen (third) masts, while lateen topsails are shown upon the same masts.

Now the customary rig in vessels of this period having four masts was to carry lateens upon both the mizzen and bonaventure mizzen. Lateen topsails have always seemed to us to be rather apocryphal. Of course it is possible that some four-masted ships might have had square sails (courses) on the first three masts, but the weight of evidence seems to be against it. We have, however, followed the painting in this particular, because, until somebody proves the negative (which is rather a large order) the evidence of the said picture must be given due consideration.

¶ 4. Page 92. *Caravel.* Jal, both in his "Glossaire Nautique," Mémoire No. 6 and in his "Archéologie Navale," sub-title, "Caravella," labours to prove that all three of the vessels of Columbus, the *Santa Maria, Niña,* and *Pinta,* were caravels. He states that the caravel was a four-masted vessel having a square sail and square topsail on the foremost and lateen sails on the other three. In his Mémoire No. 6, p. 227 *et seq.,* he states that Columbus changed the rigging of the *Pinta* to the square rig of a round ship (nef, carrack, etc.). It is submitted that there is no proof deducible from the text of the Spanish writers who have described the vessels of the Columbus fleet, that all were caravels. In fact, Jal admits (p. 231) that the admiral called the *Santa Maria* by the generic term, "nao." That the *Santa Maria* was rigged like a nef, *i. e.,* square-rigged on fore-mast and mainmast, there is no doubt, Columbus's own narrative asserts it. Jal's allegations that this vessel was a caravel are pure assumption. There seems no good reason to doubt that the *Santa Maria* was other than the type of vessel designated by Columbus himself a "nao" or "nef" (ship).

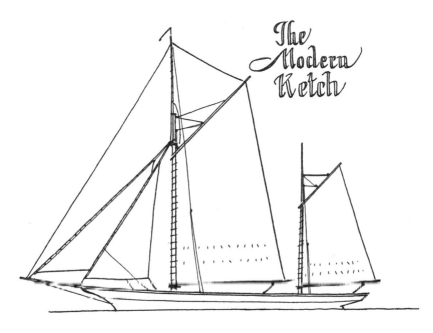

The Modern Ketch

¶ 5. Page 150. *Ketch.* The English word "catch," derived from *cache* and applied to a cargo boat, had also the meaning of chase or pursuit. It has gradually been corrupted into its present spelling of "ketch." Such a derivation obviously rejects any eastern origin of the word or of the rig, while the French word *cache* as applied to a vessel does not seem to have made its appearance until long after the word came into use in English.

In the 19th Century, after the more general adoption of fore and aft sails for pleasure craft, it was quite usual to equip yachts with square sails on the mainmast in addition to the fore and aft sails on the main and mizzen. The omission of the square sails produced the rig, now common, which is called a ketch. It is far simpler than its square-rigged ancestor, but its lineage is readily traced. No attempt has been made to differentiate between the ketch and the yawl rigs.

¶ 6. Page 182. *Mât à pible*. This is really a pole mast. Such a spar was frequently used in vessels carrying square sails, one above the other. By the term pole mast is meant one consisting of a single continuous piece of wood, not joined together from three separate pieces consisting of the lower mast, the topmast and the topgallant mast erected one upon the other, as in the majority of square-rigged masts.

A *mât à pible* had no round top, no spreaders, and no masthead cap.

This arrangement had the advantage of permitting the upper yards to be lowered until they rested upon the lower yard. Thus the canvas could be easily and quickly shortened and stowed. Having no trestle trees, crosstrees, tops, mastcaps, or rigging connected with these fittings, such a mast was very light and well suited to some types of vessels.

¶ 7. Page 194. *Top ropes*. The *drisse* has been sufficiently described in the article on the bilander where it was mentioned that one of the four sheeves in the *sep* was reserved for the top rope.

Until some indeterminate date in the 18th Century it was the universal practice to carry the top ropes employed in raising and lowering the topmasts rigged and ready for immediate use.

The standing part of the top rope made fast usually to an eye-bolt underneath the mast cap. The rope then passed down and through a sheeve or *joue de vache* at the bottom of the topmast, up again through a large and heavy metal-strapped block hanging from another eye-bolt on the other side of the mast-cap, thence down through the lubber-hole in the top of the fourth sheeve in the step and the hauling part led thence to the deck or jeer capstan if the topmast was to be hoisted into place; otherwise, when the topmast was at the cap and fid was in place, there was no strain on this rope. Later, two top ropes were usually employed, the second passing through a second sheeve in the topmast foot a little higher than the one al-

APPENDIX

ready mentioned. Two mast-cap blocks were also employed and the power was applied to each top rope by means of a tackle consisting of a treble and double block and its fall, hooked to an eye-bolt aft of the mast.

The top rope is still employed in getting the topmast into position. It used to be the custom to lower the topmast when any sort of heavy weather was expected or experienced; later the topmasts were lowered only in bad storms. Since the adoption of wire rope-rigging it is very rarely if ever that stress of weather compels the striking or lowering of these masts.

¶ 8. Pages 202 and 214. *Mât à calcet.* So called from the square block or head, *le calcet,* with which it terminated aloft.

These masts were heavy and short and were employed in the galleys and other vessels using lateen sails.

The square head was pierced with several mortises in which were placed the sheeves through which passed the halyards and other ropes.

A stay forward of the mast was not employed.

The shrouds which supported the *mâts à calcet* were different from those of ordinary ships. They were of two sorts, one used upon the galleys, set up by means of pulleys and falls instead of deadeyes and lanyards. The lower blocks of the said tackles were toggled to iron eye-bolts along the outside of the apostis. This is what was called shrouds, galley fashion. The other sort of shroud used in connection with the lateen rig consisted of a pendant fixed at the mast head, into the lower end of which pendant was turned a single block. Through this passed a runner, the standing part of the runner was hooked or toggled to the gunwale, the hauling part being equipped with a four-part tackle also hooked or toggled to the gunwale, near the end of the standing part. This is similar to the tackles originally used to supplement the shrouds and for other purposes in regular square-rigged vessels. These shrouds were never crossed with ratlines.

¶ 9. Page 243. *Superstitions.* Among sea-faring folk there are many superstitions, taboo words, and aversions. The sailors and fishermen in certain localities are most averse to the mention of a hare or a rabbit. It is considered the worst sort of bad luck to see this rodent and it is therefore never referred to except as "a furry thing." Pigs, women, and ministers are also considered unlucky objects. For some men, whether they be mariners or not, the second-named object of the trio is obviously so, but so far as the superstition goes, a woman is only an object of ill omen if she happens to be carrying an empty pail or to cross the mariner's path.

Ministers were proverbially unlucky. Their presence on a ship was claimed to bode foul weather. At sea they were never mentioned by name.

One of the most widely spread superstitions was that against beginning a voyage on a Friday.

It was also claimed that ill-chance at a launching pursued a vessel in its later career. And there was a curious superstition in early times which may account for the fact that horns were often carried on vessels as talismans. It was that no vessel could be successful unless, when it was first put into the water, there was a liberal attendance of cuckolds. An exaggerated and lofty name also presaged ill-fortune to the ship bearing it. And it was considered a fatal mistake to name a ship after an ocean or sea, as witness the verses appearing after the loss of the *Atlantic* wherein the ocean bearing that name is made to exclaim in wrath, "there shall not *two* Atlantics be."

¶ 10. Page 284. *Mizzen.* All ships carried triangular lateen mizzen courses until the latter part of the 18th Century. About this time the apex of the triangle, *i.e.,* that portion of the sail forward of the mizzenmast, was dispensed with. The after or larger part of the sail was extended upon the upper portion of the lateen mizzen yard. There was no boom. Fig. 1.)

Then the lateen yard itself, first in small vessels and a little later in large ones, gave way to the gaff, sometimes moving up and down the mizzenmast or upon a trysail mast similar to that in use in snows, sometimes suspended by chains and immovable. The sail thus extended was still called the mizzen course. (Fig. 2.)

At some time prior to the year 1770 a sail called a driver was in use, but employed only when the wind was favourable. This form of driver consisted of a narrow rectangle of cloth, of which the head, spread upon a yard, was hoisted to the peak of the mizzen yard (later of the gaff) and the foot was extended on a boom thrust out across the ship and projecting from the lee quarter. This is Falconer's description: (Fig. 3.) Darcey Lever (1808) shows a trapezoidal sail, hoisted to the peak, and with its foot extended by a boom, in a different form, what we would call a ring-tail, but which he

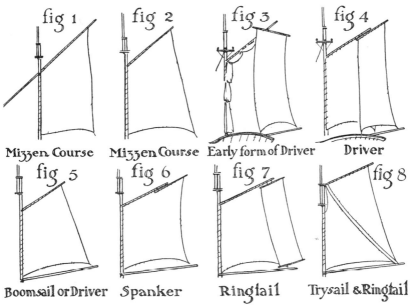

fig 1	fig 2	fig 3	fig 4
Mizzen Course	Mizzen Course	Early form of Driver	Driver
fig 5	fig 6	fig 7	fig 8
Boomsail or Driver	Spanker	Ringtail	Trysail & Ringtail

calls a driver. (Fig. 4.) Falconer also mentions a ring-tail, practically as we would understand it. (Fig. 7.)

When a boom was added it apparently caused the trapezoidal piece of canvas (formerly known as the mizzen course) to be called a driver boomsail or perhaps just plain driver. (See Steele, "Rigging & Seamanship, Practice of Sailmaking," Vol. 1, p. 118). (Fig. 5.)

Lever says:

The driver or spanker is now cut mainsail fashion and in this case it is spread by a boom. The spanker acts as a large mizzen; but as the gaff is not of sufficient squareness to spread the head (i. e., is not long enough), the after part of it (the head) is bent on the yard. [Fig. 6].

This is the earliest use that the author has been able to find of the word "spanker," a word now almost universally employed to describe the lower fore-and-aft sail carried upon the mizzenmast of ships and barks. The spanker originally was a fair-weather sail, used somewhat after the manner of studding-sails, as an enlargement of the driver and embracing partly the functions of the ringtail. It is submitted that it would be more correct to refer to the said fore-and-aft sail, extended by a gaff and a boom, as a driver, the word used to describe the fore-and-aft sail on brigs, barkentines, and brigantines, as the use of the word "mizzen," where it refers to a fore-and-aft sail, seems to be confined to a sail extended on a gaff but without a boom. Moreover, this latter term is liable to lead to confusion, because a square sail is now often carried upon the lower yard of the mizzenmast commonly known as the cross-jack, on which in early times no sail was carried. At any rate, we feel that the word "spanker" is now incorrectly used.

Another form of ring-tail is shown in Figure 8 in connection with a mizzen trysail. This combination is now in use quite generally.

A CATALOG OF SELECTED
DOVER BOOKS
IN ALL FIELDS OF INTEREST

A CATALOG OF SELECTED DOVER
BOOKS IN ALL FIELDS OF INTEREST

CONCERNING THE SPIRITUAL IN ART, Wassily Kandinsky. Pioneering work by father of abstract art. Thoughts on color theory, nature of art. Analysis of earlier masters. 12 illustrations. 80pp. of text. 5⅜ x 8½.   23411-8 Pa. $4.95

ANIMALS: 1,419 Copyright-Free Illustrations of Mammals, Birds, Fish, Insects, etc., Jim Harter (ed.). Clear wood engravings present, in extremely lifelike poses, over 1,000 species of animals. One of the most extensive pictorial sourcebooks of its kind. Captions. Index. 284pp. 9 x 12.   23766-4 Pa. $14.95

CELTIC ART: The Methods of Construction, George Bain. Simple geometric techniques for making Celtic interlacements, spirals, Kells-type initials, animals, humans, etc. Over 500 illustrations. 160pp. 9 x 12. (USO)   22923-8 Pa. $9.95

AN ATLAS OF ANATOMY FOR ARTISTS, Fritz Schider. Most thorough reference work on art anatomy in the world. Hundreds of illustrations, including selections from works by Vesalius, Leonardo, Goya, Ingres, Michelangelo, others. 593 illustrations. 192pp. 7⅛ x 10¼.   20241-0 Pa. $9.95

CELTIC HAND STROKE-BY-STROKE (Irish Half-Uncial from "The Book of Kells"): An Arthur Baker Calligraphy Manual, Arthur Baker. Complete guide to creating each letter of the alphabet in distinctive Celtic manner. Covers hand position, strokes, pens, inks, paper, more. Illustrated. 48pp. 8¼ x 11.   24336-2 Pa. $3.95

EASY ORIGAMI, John Montroll. Charming collection of 32 projects (hat, cup, pelican, piano, swan, many more) specially designed for the novice origami hobbyist. Clearly illustrated easy-to-follow instructions insure that even beginning papercrafters will achieve successful results. 48pp. 8¼ x 11.   27298-2 Pa. $3.50

THE COMPLETE BOOK OF BIRDHOUSE CONSTRUCTION FOR WOOD-WORKERS, Scott D. Campbell. Detailed instructions, illustrations, tables. Also data on bird habitat and instinct patterns. Bibliography. 3 tables. 63 illustrations in 15 figures. 48pp. 5¼ x 8½.   24407-5 Pa. $2.50

BLOOMINGDALE'S ILLUSTRATED 1886 CATALOG: Fashions, Dry Goods and Housewares, Bloomingdale Brothers. Famed merchants' extremely rare catalog depicting about 1,700 products: clothing, housewares, firearms, dry goods, jewelry, more. Invaluable for dating, identifying vintage items. Also, copyright-free graphics for artists, designers. Co-published with Henry Ford Museum & Greenfield Village. 160pp. 8¼ x 11.   25780-0 Pa. $10.95

HISTORIC COSTUME IN PICTURES, Braun & Schneider. Over 1,450 costumed figures in clearly detailed engravings—from dawn of civilization to end of 19th century. Captions. Many folk costumes. 256pp. 8⅜ x 11¾.   23150-X Pa. $12.95

CATALOG OF DOVER BOOKS

STICKLEY CRAFTSMAN FURNITURE CATALOGS, Gustav Stickley and L. & J. G. Stickley. Beautiful, functional furniture in two authentic catalogs from 1910. 594 illustrations, including 277 photos, show settles, rockers, armchairs, reclining chairs, bookcases, desks, tables. 183pp. 6½ x 9¼. 23838-5 Pa. $11.95

AMERICAN LOCOMOTIVES IN HISTORIC PHOTOGRAPHS: 1858 to 1949, Ron Ziel (ed.). A rare collection of 126 meticulously detailed official photographs, called "builder portraits," of American locomotives that majestically chronicle the rise of steam locomotive power in America. Introduction. Detailed captions. xi + 129pp. 9 x 12. 27393-8 Pa. $13.95

AMERICA'S LIGHTHOUSES: An Illustrated History, Francis Ross Holland, Jr. Delightfully written, profusely illustrated fact-filled survey of over 200 American lighthouses since 1716. History, anecdotes, technological advances, more. 240pp. 8 x 10¾. 25576-X Pa. $12.95

TOWARDS A NEW ARCHITECTURE, Le Corbusier. Pioneering manifesto by founder of "International School." Technical and aesthetic theories, views of industry, economics, relation of form to function, "mass-production split" and much more. Profusely illustrated. 320pp. 6⅛ x 9¼. (USO) 25023-7 Pa. $9.95

HOW THE OTHER HALF LIVES, Jacob Riis. Famous journalistic record, exposing poverty and degradation of New York slums around 1900, by major social reformer. 100 striking and influential photographs. 233pp. 10 x 7⅞. 22012-5 Pa. $11.95

FRUIT KEY AND TWIG KEY TO TREES AND SHRUBS, William M. Harlow. One of the handiest and most widely used identification aids. Fruit key covers 120 deciduous and evergreen species; twig key 160 deciduous species. Easily used. Over 300 photographs. 126pp. 5⅜ x 8½. 20511-8 Pa. $3.95

COMMON BIRD SONGS, Dr. Donald J. Borror. Songs of 60 most common U.S. birds: robins, sparrows, cardinals, bluejays, finches, more–arranged in order of increasing complexity. Up to 9 variations of songs of each species. Cassette and manual 99911-4 $8.95

ORCHIDS AS HOUSE PLANTS, Rebecca Tyson Northen. Grow cattleyan and many other kinds of orchids–in a window, in a case, or under artificial light. 63 illustrations. 148pp. 5⅜ x 8½. 23261-1 Pa. $5.95

MONSTER MAZES, Dave Phillips. Masterful mazes at four levels of difficulty. Avoid deadly perils and evil creatures to find magical treasures. Solutions for all 32 exciting illustrated puzzles. 48pp. 8¼ x 11. 26005-4 Pa. $2.95

MOZART'S DON GIOVANNI (DOVER OPERA LIBRETTO SERIES), Wolfgang Amadeus Mozart. Introduced and translated by Ellen H. Bleiler. Standard Italian libretto, with complete English translation. Convenient and thoroughly portable–an ideal companion for reading along with a recording or the performance itself. Introduction. List of characters. Plot summary. 121pp. 5¼ x 8½. 24944-1 Pa. $3.95

TECHNICAL MANUAL AND DICTIONARY OF CLASSICAL BALLET, Gail Grant. Defines, explains, comments on steps, movements, poses and concepts. 15-page pictorial section. Basic book for student, viewer. 127pp. 5⅜ x 8½. 21843-0 Pa. $4.95

THE CLARINET AND CLARINET PLAYING, David Pino. Lively, comprehensive work features suggestions about technique, musicianship, and musical interpretation, as well as guidelines for teaching, making your own reeds, and preparing for public performance. Includes an intriguing look at clarinet history. "A godsend," The Clarinet, Journal of the International Clarinet Society. Appendixes. 7 illus. 320pp. 5⅜ x 8½. 40270-3 Pa. $9.95

HOLLYWOOD GLAMOR PORTRAITS, John Kobal (ed.). 145 photos from 1926-49. Harlow, Gable, Bogart, Bacall; 94 stars in all. Full background on photographers, technical aspects. 160pp. 8⅜ x 11¼. 23352-9 Pa. $12.95

THE ANNOTATED CASEY AT THE BAT: A Collection of Ballads about the Mighty Casey/Third, Revised Edition, Martin Gardner (ed.). Amusing sequels and parodies of one of America's best-loved poems: Casey's Revenge, Why Casey Whiffed, Casey's Sister at the Bat, others. 256pp. 5⅜ x 8½. 28598-7 Pa. $8.95

THE RAVEN AND OTHER FAVORITE POEMS, Edgar Allan Poe. Over 40 of the author's most memorable poems: "The Bells," "Ulalume," "Israfel," "To Helen," "The Conqueror Worm," "Eldorado," "Annabel Lee," many more. Alphabetic lists of titles and first lines. 64pp. 5³⁄₁₆ x 8¼. 26685-0 Pa. $1.00

PERSONAL MEMOIRS OF U. S. GRANT, Ulysses Simpson Grant. Intelligent, deeply moving firsthand account of Civil War campaigns, considered by many the finest military memoirs ever written. Includes letters, historic photographs, maps and more. 528pp. 6⅛ x 9¼. 28587-1 Pa. $12.95

ANCIENT EGYPTIAN MATERIALS AND INDUSTRIES, A. Lucas and J. Harris. Fascinating, comprehensive, thoroughly documented text describes this ancient civilization's vast resources and the processes that incorporated them in daily life, including the use of animal products, building materials, cosmetics, perfumes and incense, fibers, glazed ware, glass and its manufacture, materials used in the mummification process, and much more. 544pp. 6⅛ x 9¼. (USO) 40446-3 Pa. $16.95

RUSSIAN STORIES/PYCCKNE PACCKA3bl: A Dual-Language Book, edited by Gleb Struve. Twelve tales by such masters as Chekhov, Tolstoy, Dostoevsky, Pushkin, others. Excellent word-for-word English translations on facing pages, plus teaching and study aids, Russian/English vocabulary, biographical/critical introductions, more. 416pp. 5⅜ x 8½. 26244-8 Pa. $9.95

PHILADELPHIA THEN AND NOW: 60 Sites Photographed in the Past and Present, Kenneth Finkel and Susan Oyama. Rare photographs of City Hall, Logan Square, Independence Hall, Betsy Ross House, other landmarks juxtaposed with contemporary views. Captures changing face of historic city. Introduction. Captions. 128pp. 8¼ x 11. 25790-8 Pa. $9.95

AIA ARCHITECTURAL GUIDE TO NASSAU AND SUFFOLK COUNTIES, LONG ISLAND, The American Institute of Architects, Long Island Chapter, and the Society for the Preservation of Long Island Antiquities. Comprehensive, well-researched and generously illustrated volume brings to life over three centuries of Long Island's great architectural heritage. More than 240 photographs with authoritative, extensively detailed captions. 176pp. 8¼ x 11. 26946-9 Pa. $14.95

NORTH AMERICAN INDIAN LIFE: Customs and Traditions of 23 Tribes, Elsie Clews Parsons (ed.). 27 fictionalized essays by noted anthropologists examine religion, customs, government, additional facets of life among the Winnebago, Crow, Zuni, Eskimo, other tribes. 480pp. 6⅛ x 9¼. 27377-6 Pa. $10.95

FRANK LLOYD WRIGHT'S DANA HOUSE, Donald Hoffmann. Pictorial essay of residential masterpiece with over 160 interior and exterior photos, plans, elevations, sketches and studies. 128pp. 9¼ x 10¾. 29120-0 Pa. $12.95

THE MALE AND FEMALE FIGURE IN MOTION: 60 Classic Photographic Sequences, Eadweard Muybridge. 60 true-action photographs of men and women walking, running, climbing, bending, turning, etc., reproduced from rare 19th-century masterpiece. vi + 121pp. 9 x 12. 24745-7 Pa. $10.95

1001 QUESTIONS ANSWERED ABOUT THE SEASHORE, N. J. Berrill and Jacquelyn Berrill. Queries answered about dolphins, sea snails, sponges, starfish, fishes, shore birds, many others. Covers appearance, breeding, growth, feeding, much more. 305pp. 5¼ x 8¼. 23366-9 Pa. $9.95

ATTRACTING BIRDS TO YOUR YARD, William J. Weber. Easy-to-follow guide offers advice on how to attract the greatest diversity of birds: birdhouses, feeders, water and waterers, much more. 96pp. 5³⁄₁₆ x 8¼. 28927-3 Pa. $2.50

MEDICINAL AND OTHER USES OF NORTH AMERICAN PLANTS: A Historical Survey with Special Reference to the Eastern Indian Tribes, Charlotte Erichsen-Brown. Chronological historical citations document 500 years of usage of plants, trees, shrubs native to eastern Canada, northeastern U.S. Also complete identifying information. 343 illustrations. 544pp. 6½ x 9¼. 25951-X Pa. $12.95

STORYBOOK MAZES, Dave Phillips. 23 stories and mazes on two-page spreads: Wizard of Oz, Treasure Island, Robin Hood, etc. Solutions. 64pp. 8¼ x 11. 23628-5 Pa. $2.95

AMERICAN NEGRO SONGS: 230 Folk Songs and Spirituals, Religious and Secular, John W. Work. This authoritative study traces the African influences of songs sung and played by black Americans at work, in church, and as entertainment. The author discusses the lyric significance of such songs as "Swing Low, Sweet Chariot," "John Henry," and others and offers the words and music for 230 songs. Bibliography. Index of Song Titles. 272pp. 6½ x 9¼. 40271-1 Pa. $9.95

MOVIE-STAR PORTRAITS OF THE FORTIES, John Kobal (ed.). 163 glamor, studio photos of 106 stars of the 1940s: Rita Hayworth, Ava Gardner, Marlon Brando, Clark Gable, many more. 176pp. 8⅜ x 11¼. 23546-7 Pa. $14.95

BENCHLEY LOST AND FOUND, Robert Benchley. Finest humor from early 30s, about pet peeves, child psychologists, post office and others. Mostly unavailable elsewhere. 73 illustrations by Peter Arno and others. 183pp. 5⅜ x 8½. 22410-4 Pa. $6.95

YEKL and THE IMPORTED BRIDEGROOM AND OTHER STORIES OF YIDDISH NEW YORK, Abraham Cahan. Film Hester Street based on Yekl (1896). Novel, other stories among first about Jewish immigrants on N.Y.'s East Side. 240pp. 5⅜ x 8½. 22427-9 Pa. $6.95

SELECTED POEMS, Walt Whitman. Generous sampling from *Leaves of Grass*. Twenty-four poems include "I Hear America Singing," "Song of the Open Road," "I Sing the Body Electric," "When Lilacs Last in the Dooryard Bloom'd," "O Captain! My Captain!"–all reprinted from an authoritative edition. Lists of titles and first lines. 128pp. 5³⁄₁₆ x 8¼. 26878-0 Pa. $1.00

THE BEST TALES OF HOFFMANN, E. T. A. Hoffmann. 10 of Hoffmann's most important stories: "Nutcracker and the King of Mice," "The Golden Flowerpot," etc. 458pp. 5⅜ x 8½. 21793-0 Pa. $9.95

FROM FETISH TO GOD IN ANCIENT EGYPT, E. A. Wallis Budge. Rich detailed survey of Egyptian conception of "God" and gods, magic, cult of animals, Osiris, more. Also, superb English translations of hymns and legends. 240 illustrations. 545pp. 5⅜ x 8½. 25803-3 Pa. $13.95

FRENCH STORIES/CONTES FRANÇAIS: A Dual-Language Book, Wallace Fowlie. Ten stories by French masters, Voltaire to Camus: "Micromegas" by Voltaire; "The Atheist's Mass" by Balzac; "Minuet" by de Maupassant; "The Guest" by Camus, six more. Excellent English translations on facing pages. Also French-English vocabulary list, exercises, more. 352pp. 5⅜ x 8½. 26443-2 Pa. $9.95

CHICAGO AT THE TURN OF THE CENTURY IN PHOTOGRAPHS: 122 Historic Views from the Collections of the Chicago Historical Society, Larry A. Viskochil. Rare large-format prints offer detailed views of City Hall, State Street, the Loop, Hull House, Union Station, many other landmarks, circa 1904-1913. Introduction. Captions. Maps. 144pp. 9⅜ x 12¼. 24656-6 Pa. $12.95

OLD BROOKLYN IN EARLY PHOTOGRAPHS, 1865-1929, William Lee Younger. Luna Park, Gravesend race track, construction of Grand Army Plaza, moving of Hotel Brighton, etc. 157 previously unpublished photographs. 165pp. 8⅞ x 11¾. 23587-4 Pa. $13.95

THE MYTHS OF THE NORTH AMERICAN INDIANS, Lewis Spence. Rich anthology of the myths and legends of the Algonquins, Iroquois, Pawnees and Sioux, prefaced by an extensive historical and ethnological commentary. 36 illustrations. 480pp. 5⅜ x 8½. 25967-6 Pa. $10.95

AN ENCYCLOPEDIA OF BATTLES: Accounts of Over 1,560 Battles from 1479 B.C. to the Present, David Eggenberger. Essential details of every major battle in recorded history from the first battle of Megiddo in 1479 B.C. to Grenada in 1984. List of Battle Maps. New Appendix covering the years 1967-1984. Index. 99 illustrations. 544pp. 6½ x 9¼. 24913-1 Pa. $16.95

SAILING ALONE AROUND THE WORLD, Captain Joshua Slocum. First man to sail around the world, alone, in small boat. One of great feats of seamanship told in delightful manner. 67 illustrations. 294pp. 5⅜ x 8½. 20326-3 Pa. $6.95

ANARCHISM AND OTHER ESSAYS, Emma Goldman. Powerful, penetrating, prophetic essays on direct action, role of minorities, prison reform, puritan hypocrisy, violence, etc. 271pp. 5⅜ x 8½. 22484-8 Pa. $7.95

MYTHS OF THE HINDUS AND BUDDHISTS, Ananda K. Coomaraswamy and Sister Nivedita. Great stories of the epics; deeds of Krishna, Shiva, taken from puranas, Vedas, folk tales; etc. 32 illustrations. 400pp. 5⅜ x 8½. 21759-0 Pa. $12.95

THE TRAUMA OF BIRTH, Otto Rank. Rank's controversial thesis that anxiety neurosis is caused by profound psychological trauma which occurs at birth. 256pp. 5⅜ x 8½. 27974-X Pa. $7.95

A THEOLOGICO-POLITICAL TREATISE, Benedict Spinoza. Also contains unfinished Political Treatise. Great classic on religious liberty, theory of government on common consent. R. Elwes translation. Total of 421pp. 5⅜ x 8½. 20249-6 Pa. $9.95

MY BONDAGE AND MY FREEDOM, Frederick Douglass. Born a slave, Douglass became outspoken force in antislavery movement. The best of Douglass' autobiographies. Graphic description of slave life. 464pp. 5⅜ x 8½. 22457-0 Pa. $8.95

FOLLOWING THE EQUATOR: A Journey Around the World, Mark Twain. Fascinating humorous account of 1897 voyage to Hawaii, Australia, India, New Zealand, etc. Ironic, bemused reports on peoples, customs, climate, flora and fauna, politics, much more. 197 illustrations. 720pp. 5⅜ x 8½. 26113-1 Pa. $15.95

THE PEOPLE CALLED SHAKERS, Edward D. Andrews. Definitive study of Shakers: origins, beliefs, practices, dances, social organization, furniture and crafts, etc. 33 illustrations. 351pp. 5⅜ x 8½. 21081-2 Pa. $8.95

THE MYTHS OF GREECE AND ROME, H. A. Guerber. A classic of mythology, generously illustrated, long prized for its simple, graphic, accurate retelling of the principal myths of Greece and Rome, and for its commentary on their origins and significance. With 64 illustrations by Michelangelo, Raphael, Titian, Rubens, Canova, Bernini and others. 480pp. 5⅜ x 8½. 27584-1 Pa. $9.95

PSYCHOLOGY OF MUSIC, Carl E. Seashore. Classic work discusses music as a medium from psychological viewpoint. Clear treatment of physical acoustics, auditory apparatus, sound perception, development of musical skills, nature of musical feeling, host of other topics. 88 figures. 408pp. 5⅜ x 8½. 21851-1 Pa. $11.95

THE PHILOSOPHY OF HISTORY, Georg W. Hegel. Great classic of Western thought develops concept that history is not chance but rational process, the evolution of freedom. 457pp. 5⅜ x 8½. 20112-0 Pa. $9.95

THE BOOK OF TEA, Kakuzo Okakura. Minor classic of the Orient: entertaining, charming explanation, interpretation of traditional Japanese culture in terms of tea ceremony. 94pp. 5⅜ x 8½. 20070-1 Pa. $3.95

LIFE IN ANCIENT EGYPT, Adolf Erman. Fullest, most thorough, detailed older account with much not in more recent books, domestic life, religion, magic, medicine, commerce, much more. Many illustrations reproduce tomb paintings, carvings, hieroglyphs, etc. 597pp. 5⅜ x 8½. 22632-8 Pa. $12.95

SUNDIALS, Their Theory and Construction, Albert Waugh. Far and away the best, most thorough coverage of ideas, mathematics concerned, types, construction, adjusting anywhere. Simple, nontechnical treatment allows even children to build several of these dials. Over 100 illustrations. 230pp. 5⅜ x 8½. 22947-5 Pa. $8.95

THEORETICAL HYDRODYNAMICS, L. M. Milne-Thomson. Classic exposition of the mathematical theory of fluid motion, applicable to both hydrodynamics and aerodynamics. Over 600 exercises. 768pp. 6⅛ x 9¼. 68970-0 Pa. $20.95

SONGS OF EXPERIENCE: Facsimile Reproduction with 26 Plates in Full Color, William Blake. 26 full-color plates from a rare 1826 edition. Includes "TheTyger," "London," "Holy Thursday," and other poems. Printed text of poems. 48pp. 5¼ x 7. 24636-1 Pa. $4.95

OLD-TIME VIGNETTES IN FULL COLOR, Carol Belanger Grafton (ed.). Over 390 charming, often sentimental illustrations, selected from archives of Victorian graphics—pretty women posing, children playing, food, flowers, kittens and puppies, smiling cherubs, birds and butterflies, much more. All copyright-free. 48pp. 9¼ x 12¼. 27269-9 Pa. $7.95

PERSPECTIVE FOR ARTISTS, Rex Vicat Cole. Depth, perspective of sky and sea, shadows, much more, not usually covered. 391 diagrams, 81 reproductions of drawings and paintings. 279pp. 5⅜ x 8½. 22487-2 Pa. $7.95

DRAWING THE LIVING FIGURE, Joseph Sheppard. Innovative approach to artistic anatomy focuses on specifics of surface anatomy, rather than muscles and bones. Over 170 drawings of live models in front, back and side views, and in widely varying poses. Accompanying diagrams. 177 illustrations. Introduction. Index. 144pp. 8⅜ x11¼. 26723-7 Pa. $8.95

GOTHIC AND OLD ENGLISH ALPHABETS: 100 Complete Fonts, Dan X. Solo. Add power, elegance to posters, signs, other graphics with 100 stunning copyright-free alphabets: Blackstone, Dolbey, Germania, 97 more–including many lower-case, numerals, punctuation marks. 104pp. 8⅛ x 11. 24695-7 Pa. $8.95

HOW TO DO BEADWORK, Mary White. Fundamental book on craft from simple projects to five-bead chains and woven works. 106 illustrations. 142pp. 5⅜ x 8. 20697-1 Pa. $5.95

THE BOOK OF WOOD CARVING, Charles Marshall Sayers. Finest book for beginners discusses fundamentals and offers 34 designs. "Absolutely first rate . . . well thought out and well executed."–E. J. Tangerman. 118pp. 7¾ x 10⅝. 23654-4 Pa. $7.95

ILLUSTRATED CATALOG OF CIVIL WAR MILITARY GOODS: Union Army Weapons, Insignia, Uniform Accessories, and Other Equipment, Schuyler, Hartley, and Graham. Rare, profusely illustrated 1846 catalog includes Union Army uniform and dress regulations, arms and ammunition, coats, insignia, flags, swords, rifles, etc. 226 illustrations. 160pp. 9 x 12. 24939-5 Pa. $10.95

WOMEN'S FASHIONS OF THE EARLY 1900s: An Unabridged Republication of "New York Fashions, 1909," National Cloak & Suit Co. Rare catalog of mail-order fashions documents women's and children's clothing styles shortly after the turn of the century. Captions offer full descriptions, prices. Invaluable resource for fashion, costume historians. Approximately 725 illustrations. 128pp. 8⅜ x 11¼. 27276-1 Pa. $11.95

THE 1912 AND 1915 GUSTAV STICKLEY FURNITURE CATALOGS, Gustav Stickley. With over 200 detailed illustrations and descriptions, these two catalogs are essential reading and reference materials and identification guides for Stickley furniture. Captions cite materials, dimensions and prices. 112pp. 6½ x 9¼. 26676-1 Pa. $9.95

EARLY AMERICAN LOCOMOTIVES, John H. White, Jr. Finest locomotive engravings from early 19th century: historical (1804–74), main-line (after 1870), special, foreign, etc. 147 plates. 142pp. 11⅜ x 8¼. 22772-3 Pa. $10.95

THE TALL SHIPS OF TODAY IN PHOTOGRAPHS, Frank O. Braynard. Lavishly illustrated tribute to nearly 100 majestic contemporary sailing vessels: Amerigo Vespucci, Clearwater, Constitution, Eagle, Mayflower, Sea Cloud, Victory, many more. Authoritative captions provide statistics, background on each ship. 190 black-and-white photographs and illustrations. Introduction. 128pp. 8⅞ x 11¾. 27163-3 Pa. $14.95

LITTLE BOOK OF EARLY AMERICAN CRAFTS AND TRADES, Peter Stockham (ed.). 1807 children's book explains crafts and trades: baker, hatter, cooper, potter, and many others. 23 copperplate illustrations. 140pp. 4⅝ x 6.
23336-7 Pa. $4.95

VICTORIAN FASHIONS AND COSTUMES FROM HARPER'S BAZAR, 1867–1898, Stella Blum (ed.). Day costumes, evening wear, sports clothes, shoes, hats, other accessories in over 1,000 detailed engravings. 320pp. 9⅜ x 12¼.
22990-4 Pa. $15.95

GUSTAV STICKLEY, THE CRAFTSMAN, Mary Ann Smith. Superb study surveys broad scope of Stickley's achievement, especially in architecture. Design philosophy, rise and fall of the Craftsman empire, descriptions and floor plans for many Craftsman houses, more. 86 black-and-white halftones. 31 line illustrations. Introduction 208pp. 6½ x 9¼. 27210-9 Pa. $9.95

THE LONG ISLAND RAIL ROAD IN EARLY PHOTOGRAPHS, Ron Ziel. Over 220 rare photos, informative text document origin (1844) and development of rail service on Long Island. Vintage views of early trains, locomotives, stations, passengers, crews, much more. Captions. 8⅞ x 11¾. 26301-0 Pa. $13.95

VOYAGE OF THE LIBERDADE, Joshua Slocum. Great 19th-century mariner's thrilling, first-hand account of the wreck of his ship off South America, the 35-foot boat he built from the wreckage, and its remarkable voyage home. 128pp. 5⅜ x 8½.
40022-0 Pa. $4.95

TEN BOOKS ON ARCHITECTURE, Vitruvius. The most important book ever written on architecture. Early Roman aesthetics, technology, classical orders, site selection, all other aspects. Morgan translation. 331pp. 5⅜ x 8½. 20645-9 Pa. $8.95

THE HUMAN FIGURE IN MOTION, Eadweard Muybridge. More than 4,500 stopped-action photos, in action series, showing undraped men, women, children jumping, lying down, throwing, sitting, wrestling, carrying, etc. 390pp. 7⅞ x 10⅝.
20204-6 Clothbd. $27.95

TREES OF THE EASTERN AND CENTRAL UNITED STATES AND CANADA, William M. Harlow. Best one-volume guide to 140 trees. Full descriptions, woodlore, range, etc. Over 600 illustrations. Handy size. 288pp. 4½ x 6⅜.
20395-6 Pa. $6.95

SONGS OF WESTERN BIRDS, Dr. Donald J. Borror. Complete song and call repertoire of 60 western species, including flycatchers, juncoes, cactus wrens, many more–includes fully illustrated booklet. Cassette and manual 99913-0 $8.95

GROWING AND USING HERBS AND SPICES, Milo Miloradovich. Versatile handbook provides all the information needed for cultivation and use of all the herbs and spices available in North America. 4 illustrations. Index. Glossary. 236pp. 5⅜ x 8½.
25058-X Pa. $7.95

BIG BOOK OF MAZES AND LABYRINTHS, Walter Shepherd. 50 mazes and labyrinths in all–classical, solid, ripple, and more–in one great volume. Perfect inexpensive puzzler for clever youngsters. Full solutions. 112pp. 8⅛ x 11.
22951-3 Pa. $5.95

PIANO TUNING, J. Cree Fischer. Clearest, best book for beginner, amateur. Simple repairs, raising dropped notes, tuning by easy method of flattened fifths. No previous skills needed. 4 illustrations. 201pp. 5⅜ x 8½. 23267-0 Pa. $6.95

HINTS TO SINGERS, Lillian Nordica. Selecting the right teacher, developing confidence, overcoming stage fright, and many other important skills receive thoughtful discussion in this indispensible guide, written by a world-famous diva of four decades' experience. 96pp. 5³/₈ x 8¹/₂. 40094-8 Pa. $4.95

THE COMPLETE NONSENSE OF EDWARD LEAR, Edward Lear. All nonsense limericks, zany alphabets, Owl and Pussycat, songs, nonsense botany, etc., illustrated by Lear. Total of 320pp. 5⅜ x 8½. (USO) 20167-8 Pa. $7.95

VICTORIAN PARLOUR POETRY: An Annotated Anthology, Michael R. Turner. 117 gems by Longfellow, Tennyson, Browning, many lesser-known poets. "The Village Blacksmith," "Curfew Must Not Ring Tonight," "Only a Baby Small," dozens more, often difficult to find elsewhere. Index of poets, titles, first lines. xxiii + 325pp. 5⅝ x 8¼. 27044-0 Pa. $8.95

DUBLINERS, James Joyce. Fifteen stories offer vivid, tightly focused observations of the lives of Dublin's poorer classes. At least one, "The Dead," is considered a masterpiece. Reprinted complete and unabridged from standard edition. 160pp. 5³⁄₁₆ x 8¼. 26870-5 Pa. $1.00

GREAT WEIRD TALES: 14 Stories by Lovecraft, Blackwood, Machen and Others, S. T. Joshi (ed.). 14 spellbinding tales, including "The Sin Eater," by Fiona McLeod, "The Eye Above the Mantel," by Frank Belknap Long, as well as renowned works by R. H. Barlow, Lord Dunsany, Arthur Machen, W. C. Morrow and eight other masters of the genre. 256pp. 5⅜ x 8½. (USO) 40436-6 Pa. $8.95

THE BOOK OF THE SACRED MAGIC OF ABRAMELIN THE MAGE, translated by S. MacGregor Mathers. Medieval manuscript of ceremonial magic. Basic document in Aleister Crowley, Golden Dawn groups. 268pp. 5⅜ x 8½. 23211-5 Pa. $9.95

NEW RUSSIAN-ENGLISH AND ENGLISH-RUSSIAN DICTIONARY, M. A. O'Brien. This is a remarkably handy Russian dictionary, containing a surprising amount of information, including over 70,000 entries. 366pp. 4½ x 6⅛. 20208-9 Pa. $10.95

HISTORIC HOMES OF THE AMERICAN PRESIDENTS, Second, Revised Edition, Irvin Haas. A traveler's guide to American Presidential homes, most open to the public, depicting and describing homes occupied by every American President from George Washington to George Bush. With visiting hours, admission charges, travel routes. 175 photographs. Index. 160pp. 8¼ x 11. 26751-2 Pa. $11.95

NEW YORK IN THE FORTIES, Andreas Feininger. 162 brilliant photographs by the well-known photographer, formerly with *Life* magazine. Commuters, shoppers, Times Square at night, much else from city at its peak. Captions by John von Hartz. 181pp. 9¼ x 10¾. 23585-8 Pa. $13.95

INDIAN SIGN LANGUAGE, William Tomkins. Over 525 signs developed by Sioux and other tribes. Written instructions and diagrams. Also 290 pictographs. 111pp. 6⅛ x 9¼. 22029-X Pa. $3.95

CATALOG OF DOVER BOOKS

ANATOMY: A Complete Guide for Artists, Joseph Sheppard. A master of figure drawing shows artists how to render human anatomy convincingly. Over 460 illustrations. 224pp. 8⅜ x 11¼. 27279-6 Pa. $11.95

MEDIEVAL CALLIGRAPHY: Its History and Technique, Marc Drogin. Spirited history, comprehensive instruction manual covers 13 styles (ca. 4th century thru 15th). Excellent photographs; directions for duplicating medieval techniques with modern tools. 224pp. 8⅜ x 11¼. 26142-5 Pa. $12.95

DRIED FLOWERS: How to Prepare Them, Sarah Whitlock and Martha Rankin. Complete instructions on how to use silica gel, meal and borax, perlite aggregate, sand and borax, glycerine and water to create attractive permanent flower arrangements. 12 illustrations. 32pp. 5⅜ x 8½. 21802-3 Pa. $1.00

EASY-TO-MAKE BIRD FEEDERS FOR WOODWORKERS, Scott D. Campbell. Detailed, simple-to-use guide for designing, constructing, caring for and using feeders. Text, illustrations for 12 classic and contemporary designs. 96pp. 5⅜ x 8½. 25847-5 Pa. $3.95

SCOTTISH WONDER TALES FROM MYTH AND LEGEND, Donald A. Mackenzie. 16 lively tales tell of giants rumbling down mountainsides, of a magic wand that turns stone pillars into warriors, of gods and goddesses, evil hags, powerful forces and more. 240pp. 5⅜ x 8½. 29677-6 Pa. $6.95

THE HISTORY OF UNDERCLOTHES, C. Willett Cunnington and Phyllis Cunnington. Fascinating, well-documented survey covering six centuries of English undergarments, enhanced with over 100 illustrations: 12th-century laced-up bodice, footed long drawers (1795), 19th-century bustles, 19th-century corsets for men, Victorian "bust improvers," much more. 272pp. 5⅝ x 8¼. 27124-2 Pa. $9.95

ARTS AND CRAFTS FURNITURE: The Complete Brooks Catalog of 1912, Brooks Manufacturing Co. Photos and detailed descriptions of more than 150 now very collectible furniture designs from the Arts and Crafts movement depict davenports, settees, buffets, desks, tables, chairs, bedsteads, dressers and more, all built of solid, quarter-sawed oak. Invaluable for students and enthusiasts of antiques, Americana and the decorative arts. 80pp. 6½ x 9¼. 27471-3 Pa. $8.95

WILBUR AND ORVILLE: A Biography of the Wright Brothers, Fred Howard. Definitive, crisply written study tells the full story of the brothers' lives and work. A vividly written biography, unparalleled in scope and color, that also captures the spirit of an extraordinary era. 560pp. 6⅛ x 9¼. 40297-5 Pa. $17.95

THE ARTS OF THE SAILOR: Knotting, Splicing and Ropework, Hervey Garrett Smith. Indispensable shipboard reference covers tools, basic knots and useful hitches; handsewing and canvas work, more. Over 100 illustrations. Delightful reading for sea lovers. 256pp. 5⅜ x 8½. 26440-8 Pa. $8.95

FRANK LLOYD WRIGHT'S FALLINGWATER: The House and Its History, Second, Revised Edition, Donald Hoffmann. A total revision–both in text and illustrations–of the standard document on Fallingwater, the boldest, most personal architectural statement of Wright's mature years, updated with valuable new material from the recently opened Frank Lloyd Wright Archives. "Fascinating"–*The New York Times*. 116 illustrations. 128pp. 9¼ x 10¾. 27430-6 Pa. $12.95

PHOTOGRAPHIC SKETCHBOOK OF THE CIVIL WAR, Alexander Gardner. 100 photos taken on field during the Civil War. Famous shots of Manassas Harper's Ferry, Lincoln, Richmond, slave pens, etc. 244pp. 10⅝ x 8¼. 22731-6 Pa. $10.95

FIVE ACRES AND INDEPENDENCE, Maurice G. Kains. Great back-to-the-land classic explains basics of self-sufficient farming. The one book to get. 95 illustrations. 397pp. 5⅜ x 8½. 20974-1 Pa. $7.95

SONGS OF EASTERN BIRDS, Dr. Donald J. Borror. Songs and calls of 60 species most common to eastern U.S.: warblers, woodpeckers, flycatchers, thrushes, larks, many more in high-quality recording. Cassette and manual 99912-2 $9.95

A MODERN HERBAL, Margaret Grieve. Much the fullest, most exact, most useful compilation of herbal material. Gigantic alphabetical encyclopedia, from aconite to zedoary, gives botanical information, medical properties, folklore, economic uses, much else. Indispensable to serious reader. 161 illustrations. 888pp. 6½ x 9¼. 2-vol. set. (USO) Vol. I: 22798-7 Pa. $9.95
Vol. II: 22799-5 Pa. $9.95

HIDDEN TREASURE MAZE BOOK, Dave Phillips. Solve 34 challenging mazes accompanied by heroic tales of adventure. Evil dragons, people-eating plants, blood-thirsty giants, many more dangerous adversaries lurk at every twist and turn. 34 mazes, stories, solutions. 48pp. 8¼ x 11. 24566-7 Pa. $2.95

LETTERS OF W. A. MOZART, Wolfgang A. Mozart. Remarkable letters show bawdy wit, humor, imagination, musical insights, contemporary musical world; includes some letters from Leopold Mozart. 276pp. 5⅜ x 8½. 22859-2 Pa. $7.95

BASIC PRINCIPLES OF CLASSICAL BALLET, Agrippina Vaganova. Great Russian theoretician, teacher explains methods for teaching classical ballet. 118 illus-trations. 175pp. 5⅜ x 8½. 22036-2 Pa. $5.95

THE JUMPING FROG, Mark Twain. Revenge edition. The original story of The Celebrated Jumping Frog of Calaveras County, a hapless French translation, and Twain's hilarious "retranslation" from the French. 12 illustrations. 66pp. 5⅜ x 8½. 22686-7 Pa. $3.95

BEST REMEMBERED POEMS, Martin Gardner (ed.). The 126 poems in this superb collection of 19th- and 20th-century British and American verse range from Shelley's "To a Skylark" to the impassioned "Renascence" of Edna St. Vincent Millay and to Edward Lear's whimsical "The Owl and the Pussycat." 224pp. 5⅜ x 8½. 27165-X Pa. $5.95

COMPLETE SONNETS, William Shakespeare. Over 150 exquisite poems deal with love, friendship, the tyranny of time, beauty's evanescence, death and other themes in language of remarkable power, precision and beauty. Glossary of archaic terms. 80pp. 5³⁄₁₆ x 8¼. 26686-9 Pa. $1.00

BODIES IN A BOOKSHOP, R. T. Campbell. Challenging mystery of blackmail and murder with ingenious plot and superbly drawn characters. In the best tradition of British suspense fiction. 192pp. 5⅜ x 8½. 24720-1 Pa. $6.95

THE WIT AND HUMOR OF OSCAR WILDE, Alvin Redman (ed.). More than 1,000 ripostes, paradoxes, wisecracks: Work is the curse of the drinking classes; I can resist everything except temptation; etc. 258pp. 5⅜ x 8½. 20602-5 Pa. $6.95

SHAKESPEARE LEXICON AND QUOTATION DICTIONARY, Alexander Schmidt. Full definitions, locations, shades of meaning in every word in plays and poems. More than 50,000 exact quotations. 1,485pp. 6½ x 9¼. 2-vol. set.
Vol. 1: 22726-X Pa. $17.95
Vol. 2: 22727-8 Pa. $17.95

SELECTED POEMS, Emily Dickinson. Over 100 best-known, best-loved poems by one of America's foremost poets, reprinted from authoritative early editions. No comparable edition at this price. Index of first lines. 64pp. 5³⁄₁₆ x 8¼. 26466-1 Pa. $1.00

THE INSIDIOUS DR. FU-MANCHU, Sax Rohmer. The first of the popular mystery series introduces a pair of English detectives to their archnemesis, the diabolical Dr. Fu-Manchu. Flavorful atmosphere, fast-paced action, and colorful characters enliven this classic of the genre. 208pp. 5³⁄₁₆ x 8¼. 29898-1 Pa. $2.00

THE MALLEUS MALEFICARUM OF KRAMER AND SPRENGER, translated by Montague Summers. Full text of most important witchhunter's "bible," used by both Catholics and Protestants. 278pp. 6⅝ x 10. 22802-9 Pa. $12.95

SPANISH STORIES/CUENTOS ESPAÑOLES: A Dual-Language Book, Angel Flores (ed.). Unique format offers 13 great stories in Spanish by Cervantes, Borges, others. Faithful English translations on facing pages. 352pp. 5⅜ x 8½. 25399-6 Pa. $8.95

GARDEN CITY, LONG ISLAND, IN EARLY PHOTOGRAPHS, 1869–1919, Mildred H. Smith. Handsome treasury of 118 vintage pictures, accompanied by carefully researched captions, document the Garden City Hotel fire (1899), the Vanderbilt Cup Race (1908), the first airmail flight departing from the Nassau Boulevard Aerodrome (1911), and much more. 96pp. 8⁷⁄₈ x 11³⁄₄. 40669-5 Pa. $12.95

OLD QUEENS, N.Y., IN EARLY PHOTOGRAPHS, Vincent F. Seyfried and William Asadorian. Over 160 rare photographs of Maspeth, Jamaica, Jackson Heights, and other areas. Vintage views of DeWitt Clinton mansion, 1939 World's Fair and more. Captions. 192pp. 8⅞ x 11. 26358-4 Pa. $12.95

CAPTURED BY THE INDIANS: 15 Firsthand Accounts, 1750-1870, Frederick Drimmer. Astounding true historical accounts of grisly torture, bloody conflicts, relentless pursuits, miraculous escapes and more, by people who lived to tell the tale. 384pp. 5⅜ x 8½. 24901-8 Pa. $8.95

THE WORLD'S GREAT SPEECHES (Fourth Enlarged Edition), Lewis Copeland, Lawrence W. Lamm, and Stephen J. McKenna. Nearly 300 speeches provide public speakers with a wealth of updated quotes and inspiration–from Pericles' funeral oration and William Jennings Bryan's "Cross of Gold Speech" to Malcolm X's powerful words on the Black Revolution and Earl of Spenser's tribute to his sister, Diana, Princess of Wales. 944pp. 5⅜ x 8⅜. 40903-1 Pa. $15.95

THE BOOK OF THE SWORD, Sir Richard F. Burton. Great Victorian scholar/adventurer's eloquent, erudite history of the "queen of weapons"–from prehistory to early Roman Empire. Evolution and development of early swords, variations (sabre, broadsword, cutlass, scimitar, etc.), much more. 336pp. 6⅛ x 9¼. 25434-8 Pa. $9.95

AUTOBIOGRAPHY: The Story of My Experiments with Truth, Mohandas K. Gandhi. Boyhood, legal studies, purification, the growth of the Satyagraha (nonviolent protest) movement. Critical, inspiring work of the man responsible for the freedom of India. 480pp. 5⅜ x 8½. (USO) 24593-4 Pa. $8.95

CELTIC MYTHS AND LEGENDS, T. W. Rolleston. Masterful retelling of Irish and Welsh stories and tales. Cuchulain, King Arthur, Deirdre, the Grail, many more. First paperback edition. 58 full-page illustrations. 512pp. 5⅜ x 8½. 26507-2 Pa. $9.95

THE PRINCIPLES OF PSYCHOLOGY, William James. Famous long course complete, unabridged. Stream of thought, time perception, memory, experimental methods; great work decades ahead of its time. 94 figures. 1,391pp. 5⅜ x 8½. 2-vol. set.
Vol. I: 20381-6 Pa. $13.95
Vol. II: 20382-4 Pa. $14.95

THE WORLD AS WILL AND REPRESENTATION, Arthur Schopenhauer. Definitive English translation of Schopenhauer's life work, correcting more than 1,000 errors, omissions in earlier translations. Translated by E. F. J. Payne. Total of 1,269pp. 5⅜ x 8½. 2-vol. set. Vol. 1: 21761-2 Pa. $12.95
Vol. 2: 21762-0 Pa. $12.95

MAGIC AND MYSTERY IN TIBET, Madame Alexandra David-Neel. Experiences among lamas, magicians, sages, sorcerers, Bonpa wizards. A true psychic discovery. 32 illustrations. 321pp. 5⅜ x 8½. (USO) 22682-4 Pa. $9.95

THE EGYPTIAN BOOK OF THE DEAD, E. A. Wallis Budge. Complete reproduction of Ani's papyrus, finest ever found. Full hieroglyphic text, interlinear transliteration, word-for-word translation, smooth translation. 533pp. 6½ x 9¼.
21866-X Pa. $11.95

MATHEMATICS FOR THE NONMATHEMATICIAN, Morris Kline. Detailed, college-level treatment of mathematics in cultural and historical context, with numerous exercises. Recommended Reading Lists. Tables. Numerous figures. 641pp. 5⅜ x 8½.
24823-2 Pa. $11.95

PROBABILISTIC METHODS IN THE THEORY OF STRUCTURES, Isaac Elishakoff. Well-written introduction covers the elements of the theory of probability from two or more random variables, the reliability of such multivariable structures, the theory of random function, Monte Carlo methods of treating problems incapable of exact solution, and more. Examples. 502pp. 5⅜ x 8½. 40691-1 Pa. $16.95

THE RIME OF THE ANCIENT MARINER, Gustave Doré, S. T. Coleridge. Doré's finest work; 34 plates capture moods, subtleties of poem. Flawless full-size reproductions printed on facing pages with authoritative text of poem. "Beautiful. Simply beautiful."–*Publisher's Weekly.* 77pp. 9¼ x 12. 22305-1 Pa. $7.95

NORTH AMERICAN INDIAN DESIGNS FOR ARTISTS AND CRAFTSPEOPLE, Eva Wilson. Over 360 authentic copyright-free designs adapted from Navajo blankets, Hopi pottery, Sioux buffalo hides, more. Geometrics, symbolic figures, plant and animal motifs, etc. 128pp. 8⅜ x 11. (EUK) 25341-4 Pa. $8.95

SCULPTURE: Principles and Practice, Louis Slobodkin. Step-by-step approach to clay, plaster, metals, stone; classical and modern. 253 drawings, photos. 255pp. 8⅛ x 11.
22960-2 Pa. $11.95

THE INFLUENCE OF SEA POWER UPON HISTORY, 1660–1783, A. T. Mahan. Influential classic of naval history and tactics still used as text in war colleges. First paperback edition. 4 maps. 24 battle plans. 640pp. 5⅜ x 8½.   25509-3 Pa. $14.95

THE STORY OF THE TITANIC AS TOLD BY ITS SURVIVORS, Jack Winocour (ed.). What it was really like. Panic, despair, shocking inefficiency, and a little heroism. More thrilling than any fictional account. 26 illustrations. 320pp. 5⅜ x 8½.
20610-6 Pa. $8.95

FAIRY AND FOLK TALES OF THE IRISH PEASANTRY, William Butler Yeats (ed.). Treasury of 64 tales from the twilight world of Celtic myth and legend: "The Soul Cages," "The Kildare Pooka," "King O'Toole and his Goose," many more. Introduction and Notes by W. B. Yeats. 352pp. 5⅜ x 8½.   26941-8 Pa. $8.95

BUDDHIST MAHAYANA TEXTS, E. B. Cowell and Others (eds.). Superb, accurate translations of basic documents in Mahayana Buddhism, highly important in history of religions. The Buddha-karita of Asvaghosha, Larger Sukhavativyuha, more. 448pp. 5⅜ x 8½.   25552-2 Pa. $12.95

ONE TWO THREE . . . INFINITY: Facts and Speculations of Science, George Gamow. Great physicist's fascinating, readable overview of contemporary science: number theory, relativity, fourth dimension, entropy, genes, atomic structure, much more. 128 illustrations. Index. 352pp. 5⅜ x 8½.   25664-2 Pa. $8.95

EXPERIMENTATION AND MEASUREMENT, W. J. Youden. Introductory manual explains laws of measurement in simple terms and offers tips for achieving accuracy and minimizing errors. Mathematics of measurement, use of instruments, experimenting with machines. 1994 edition. Foreword. Preface. Introduction. Epilogue. Selected Readings. Glossary. Index. Tables and figures. 128pp. 5³⁄₈ x 8¹⁄₂.
40451-X Pa. $6.95

DALÍ ON MODERN ART: The Cuckolds of Antiquated Modern Art, Salvador Dalí. Influential painter skewers modern art and its practitioners. Outrageous evaluations of Picasso, Cézanne, Turner, more. 15 renderings of paintings discussed. 44 calligraphic decorations by Dalí. 96pp. 5⅜ x 8½. (USO)   29220-7 Pa. $5.95

ANTIQUE PLAYING CARDS: A Pictorial History, Henry René D'Allemagne. Over 900 elaborate, decorative images from rare playing cards (14th–20th centuries): Bacchus, death, dancing dogs, hunting scenes, royal coats of arms, players cheating, much more. 96pp. 9¼ x 12¼.   29265-7 Pa. $12.95

MAKING FURNITURE MASTERPIECES: 30 Projects with Measured Drawings, Franklin H. Gottshall. Step-by-step instructions, illustrations for constructing handsome, useful pieces, among them a Sheraton desk, Chippendale chair, Spanish desk, Queen Anne table and a William and Mary dressing mirror. 224pp. 8⅛ x 11¼.
29338-6 Pa. $13.95

THE FOSSIL BOOK: A Record of Prehistoric Life, Patricia V. Rich et al. Profusely illustrated definitive guide covers everything from single-celled organisms and dinosaurs to birds and mammals and the interplay between climate and man. Over 1,500 illustrations. 760pp. 7½ x 10⅛.   29371-8 Pa. $29.95

Prices subject to change without notice.

Available at your book dealer or write for free catalog to Dept. GI, Dover Publications, Inc., 31 East 2nd St., Mineola, N.Y. 11501. Dover publishes more than 500 books each year on science, elementary and advanced mathematics, biology, music, art, literary history, social sciences and other areas.

8/05